I love Australia

A helpful and individual travel guide to make the best of your time in Australia. Let the adventure begin!

By S. L. Giger aka SwissMiss on Tour

A quote I found somewhere in Melbourne:

Never refuse an invitation, never resist the unfamiliar, never fail to be polite and never outstay the welcome. Just keep your mind open and suck in the experience. And if it hurts, you know what? It's probably worth it.
- Alex Garland

Copyright © 2018 Seraina Giger
All rights reserved.
ISBN: 9781726691192
Cover: Germancreative from Fiverr and S. L. Giger
Conact: Seraina Giger, swissmissstories@gmail.com

Receive a free packing list

Never forget anything important ever again and don't waste unnecessary time with packing. Send an e-mailt with the subject: **packing list** and receive a free packing list along with a sample of my Thailand travel guide.

Send the e-mail to swissmissstories@gmail.com and receive your free gift.

Content

Receive a free packing list 3
10 Reasons why you can look forward to your Australia adventure in case you aren't entirely convinced yet 11
About the author of this travel guide 13
1 Australia Highlights... 17
2 Things to consider before your Australia trip 21
   2.1 Your visa 21
   2.2 How to have an agreeable flight 22
   2.3 Important knowledge for your gap-year............... 23
      2.3.1 How to pack for long-term travel 25
      2.3.2 Which Australian sim card should you buy?.. 26
      2.3.3 How to find work on a work and travel visa. 27
      2.3.4 How to open up a bank account in Australia and get a social security number 29
      2.3.5 How to spend your nights in Australia........... 31
      2.3.6 Buying a car vs. renting a car 34
   2.4 Driving on the other side of the road................... 37
   2.5 How to navigate in Australia.................................. 37
3 Travel routes for two to three weeks of vacations 39
   3.1 Three-week itinerary for Australia's West-Coast, the North and the Red Center.. 39
   3.2 Three-week itinerary for Australia's East-Coast and Great Ocean Road 49

4 Must see stops along the West Coast (WA) 57
4.1 Perth 58
4.1.1 How to get from the airport into the center. 58
4.1.2 What to do in Perth 60
4.2 Fremantle 66
4.3 Bunbury 68
4.4 Busselton 68
4.5 Margaret River 69
4.6 Caves and stingrays 70
4.7 Pemberton fire lookout trees 71
Warren National Park 71
Gloucester National Park 72
4.8 Denmark 72
4.9 Albany 73
4.10 Porongroup National Park 74
4.11 Wave Rock 74
4.12 Lucky Bay in Cape Le Grand National Park 76
4.13 Nambung National Park (Pinnacle Desert) 77
4.14 Kalbarri National Park 78
Pelican Feeding 81
4.15 Hamelin Pools 81
4.16 Shell Beach 82
4.17 Monkey Mia 82
4.18 Coral Bay – A beautiful beach place 84

4.19 Exmouth 84
4.20 Cape Range National Park................................85
   Yardie Creek 85
Turquoise Bay..86
4.21 Karijini National Park 86
   Visitor Center..87
   Fortescue Waterfall..88
   Weano Gorge...89
   Joffre Gorge...90
   Fortescue Falls and Fern Pool..............................90
   4.21.1 Where to continue from here?....................90
   4.21.2 How to deal with road trains 91
4.22 Port Headland 92
4.23 Broome...93
   4.23.1 What to do in Broome..................................94
4.24 First Option: Gibb River Road............................96
   Must see stops along Gibb River Road...................98
4.25 Second Option: Purnululu National Park 102
5 What to see in the Northern Territory (NT)..............103
   5.1 Darwin..103
      5.1.1 From the airport to the CBD.........................103
      5.1.2 What to do in Darwin 104
      5.1.3 How to tour the NT.......................................105
   5.2 Litchfield National Park..106

- 5.3 Murray River 107
- 5.4 Kakadu National Park 108
- 5.5 Kathrine Gorge 109
- 5.6 Mataranka 110
- 5.7 Daly Waters Pub 110
- 5.8 Devils Marbles 111
- 5.9 Wycliffe Well 111
- 5.10 Alice Springs 112
- 5.11 MacDonnell Ranges 113
- 5.12 Ayers Rock (Uluru) 113
- 5.13 Kata Tjuta (the Olgas) 114
- 5.14 Kings Canyon 115
- 5.15 Camel farm in Yulara 116
- 6 Across the South: Nullarbor Plain 117
  - 6.1 Adelaide 119
    - 6.1.1 How to get from the airport to the CBD 119
    - 6.1.2 What to do in Adelaide 119
- 7 What to do in Victoria 123
  - 7.1 Great Ocean Road 123
    - 7.1.1 Portland 123
    - 7.1.2 Mt Eccles 123
    - 7.1.3 Warrnambool 124
    - 7.1.4 Twelve Apostles 125
    - 7.1.5 Gibson Steps 125

    7.1.6 Cape Otway Lighthouse 125
  7.2 Melbourne..126
    7.2.1 How to get from the airport to the CBD.....127
    7.2.2 What to do in Melbourne..............................128
  7.3 St. Kilda...133
  7.5 Wilson's Promotory...135
  7.6 Canberra 136
8 Explore New South Wales...137
  8.1 Blue Mountains 137
  8.2 Sydney..139
    8.2.1 How to get from the airport to the CBD.....140
    8.2.2 What to see and do in Sydney........................141
  8.3 Forster 144
  8.4 Coffs Harbor 145
  8.5 Learn how to surf 147
  8.6 Byron Bay..147
9 What to see in Queensland 149
  9.1 Surfers Paradise 149
    What to do in Surfer's Paradise.............................149
  9.2 Brisbane...151
    9.2.1 How to get from the airport to the CBD.....151
    9.2.2 What to do in Brisbane..................................152
  9.3 Noosa – The Margaret River of the East Coast.153
    9.3.1 What to do in Noosa......................................153

9.4 Fraser Island 155
9.5 Sailing the Whitsundays 160
9.6 Cairns 163
    9.6.1 How to get from the airport to the center .. 163
    9.6.2 What to do in Cairns 164
9.7 Great Barrier Reef 165
9.8 Port Douglas 167
9.9 Daintree Rainforest 167
9.10 For waterfall lovers 170
10 A glance in the rearview mirror 173
Do you need more info? 176
Was this guide helpful? 176
More books by S. L. Giger aka SwissMiss on Tour 176

10 Reasons why you can look forward to your Australia adventure in case you aren't entirely convinced yet

- Australia has secluded paradise beaches.

- You will see cute koalas, kangaroos, dolphins, and whales in the wilderness.

- Australia is the country with the best coffee. You will receive beautiful coffee art creations no matter where you buy a cup of coffee.

- The cities are modern and offer interesting architecture, great museums and entertainment for anyone.

- You won't be able to stop saying "wow" once you start driving an outback road. It might lead to a stunning waterfall, a natural hot tub or high trees on which you can climb.

- People are very helpful and no matter whether your car breaks down or you arrive late at night and everything is closed, someone will help you right away.

- There are still places without Wi-Fi and phone reception which offers a nice change to our busy lives.

- Even with all the possibilities we have, and everybody having done everything already anyway; in Australia, you can still find adventure and feel like an explorer in ancient times.

- Australia has a high standard for everything. Accommodations are nice and any meal you will eat will be delicious.

- It offers something for everyone. Go hiking on spectacular cliffs, surf world class waves, enjoy serene and picturesque sunsets, sip a glass of award-winning wine, party with other life-loving people and so much more. What are you waiting for?

About the author of this travel guide

Hello!

Now, that I am finished with this guidebook I'm filled with almost as much excitement as before I started my big Australia trip. Simply re-reading about all the beautiful places and remembering the wonderful people I met made me grateful all over again that I could have so many great experiences in Down Under. But let's rewind a few years: I always loved to travel. Whether it was as a child to accompany my family to an all-inclusive beach resort or to go out into the world on my own during an exchange year in the US, I always had the urge to see and experience new places. Australia had attracted me ever since my high school time. This far-away continent on the other side of the world seemed stunningly beautiful and would offer me everything I wanted: Sunshine, the most beautiful beaches, freely hopping kangaroos and cute koalas. So, like so many other people in Germany or Switzerland I decided to do a gap year after university. Work and travel in the country of my dreams really sounded like a dream come true! Unfortunately, it's not possible to receive a work and travel visa as a Swiss person. I really envied my French and German neighbors for that! So, I decided to go for six months instead of twelve and mostly travel instead of work. I did a bit of work as well and I talked to a lot of work and travelers and woofers, so you'll find all the info you need for a positive work experience in this travel guide. However, thanks to all this time for traveling I saw A LOT of Australia and let me tell you, the vastness of the outback, the colors of the sand and the oceans (yes, there are different oceans around Australia), the animals, the hip cities and the sunsets are mesmerizing. I bought a car and explored the outback with travel buddies I met in the Australian travel forums. I rented a van with people after my car broke down (fun story as well). I did the whole East-Coast with Greyhound and all the stops you need to see. I did some group tours with the most incredible sights and lovely people and I lived one month in one of the best cities in the world; Melbourne. In short: I did it all and I loved every minute of it. I hope this travel guide can help you to create just as good of an experience for yourself. Whether it is a three-week vacation or a complete gap-year.

After Australia, I started work as a teacher in Switzerland. In my free time, I still travel whenever I can or do small trips in Switzerland or to the neighboring countries. You can read more about my other travels on my blog: www.swissmissontour.com.

Apart from this travel guide, I also write romance and fantasy novels and some other "I love…" travel guides.
But now, enjoy reading about Australia. Be sure to enjoy some sunsets for me!

For your information: In this book, I always talk about **AUD (Australian Dollars)** if there is a $-sign.

1 Australia Highlights

Many times, I have been asked what my favorite place was in Australia. However, Australia is such a versatile country that it's impossible to just name one or three highlights. Therefore, I made several lists.

Nature:

1. **Karijini NP:** Amazing gorges with rocks in beautiful reds and oranges and clear green-blue water as a contrast. The hikes there involved swimming and climbing and therefore were very entertaining. The nights on the wild campsites were beautiful and driving on the outback roads during the day was a lot of fun (although it was a torture for my car and covered everything we owned in red dust.)

2. **Litchfield NP:** Waterfalls and swimming holes, WOW!!

3. **The Blue Mountains:** so close to Sydney but such awesome views and beautiful waterfalls

4. **Whitehaven Beach** in the Whitsundays. The whole sailing trip was fun.

5. **Diving at the Great Barrier Reef**

6. **Sunsets on long, straight empty roads, surrounded by nature** (and the stars at night at these deserted places...for example in the Nullarbor and in the NT)

Beaches:

Here it's hard to make a list because I just love beaches in general. And most people would probably expect me to put Whitehaven Beach on top. You can read further down, why I didn't.

1. **Beaches in Margaret River.** Wild and beautiful and waves to surf.

2. **Bundegi Beach in Exmouth** (because it felt like we had discovered an insider spot)

3. **Esperance, Lucky Bay** (such white sand and kangaroos on the beach)

4. **Coral Bay** (such white sand and crystal-clear blue water)

5. **Whitehaven Beach** (the view from the viewing platform is probably the most spectacular one I've seen in Australia but the white beach itself is not that different from Esperance or Exmouth. Plus, we had to wear a stinger suit, and so I didn't even get in direct touch with the beautiful clear water)

Very close after that is **Cottesloe** in Perth.

Cities
1. **Melbourne**
2. **Margaret River** (wine, chocolate, cheese, nature…what more do you need?)
3. **Fremantle**
4. **Noosa** (the Margaret River of the East Coast)
5. **Albany** (very backpacker friendly, many nice, free campgrounds)
6. **Sydney**

2 Things to consider before your Australia trip

Whether you are visiting Australia for only a three-week holiday or you quit your job to go there for a year, there are lots of things to consider. Following, you find all the knowledge I found useful during my time in Australia so that you can have the best possible experience in that wonderful country.

2.1 Your visa

To find out what visa you really need, fill in the short quiz on the home affairs website (https://www.homeaffairs.gov.au/Trav/Visa-1). On the same page, you then can apply for your visa. This is free of charge, you only have to pay the standard visa fee. If you go on a normal **eVisitor (subclass 651)** tourist visa (multiple entries of 3 months in six months) you can even enter Australia for free completely.

You should get your visa before you plan anything else for your trip, just to be sure that everything will work out.

With the **Visitor visa (subclass 600)** you can enter Australia for six or twelve months as a tourist and the costs start at $140.

If you want to do work and travel you need a **working holiday visa (subclass 417)**. You are able to get this visa if you are at least 18 but not yet 31 years old, if you don't have a dependent child accompanying you at any time during your stay in Australia and if you have a passport from an eligible country. Apart from working up to 12 months, you can also study for up to four months with this visa. You must apply for your first working holiday visa while you are still outside Australia. For the working holiday visa, they might ask you to show your bank account statement which needs to show that you have at least $5000. If you don't have this money, perhaps someone in your family could lend it to you, until you have your visa. The cost of the working holiday visa starts at $440.

2.2 How to have an agreeable flight

For most people, Australia is on the other side of the globe. Down Under. Which means that you will be facing a loooong flight. To make it more agreeable, **choose an airline you like** and perhaps **add a stopover** in a city. For example, with Emirates, you can add a one- or two-night stopover in Dubai which will give you a nice break in between your flights. On the other hand, you might just want to get it over with. Then, bring something to read or have a movie marathon on the plane. Don't forget to drink plenty of water to stay hydrated and circle your feet up and down from time to time to pump enough blood through your legs.

In case you think flying to Australia is too expensive, you could also break up your flight into several legs. For example, you can find a good deal to fly to Bali and then travel cheaply from Bali to Australia with AirAsia. If you don't mind having to go through several different bookings, this might be your best option.

2.3 Important knowledge for your gap-year

If you leave your home for several months to a year, there are quite a few preparations you must think of. Here is a short checklist for what you need to consider before you get on the plane.

- Get your passport up to date. It needs to be valid for at least 6 months after leaving Australia
- Did you get your visa?
- Is your credit card valid for the whole time during your travels (you need it to book flights and hostels and rent cars)? Or will you take a travel cash pre-paid credit card?
- Who will look after your apartment or things while you are gone?

- Where can you forward your mail to? Can your parents/a good friend open important mail that might arrive while you are gone? → officially authorize someone to do it
- Have you ended all abonnements and contracts (public transport, phone, internet,...) for things you don't need during the gap year?
- Check with your insurance what is covered while you are abroad. Perhaps you need to purchase an extra travel insurance.
- Do you have to pay additional fees into a retirement fund because you won't have a salary in your home country? (That's the case in Switzerland)
- Did you get your international driver's license? It's valid for three years after receiving it.
- Do you have a good backpack (I recommend Osprey) or suitcase?
- Have you bought your plane ticket?
- Have you booked your accommodation for the first few nights?
- Have you stored all the necessary documents (CV, motivation letter to find a job, a copy of the passport) in a cloud, so that you can access it in Australia?

Those are only the things you must keep in mind before you start your journey. What can you do, once you are in Australia, to make your stay easier?

Two tips right at the start: If you are tired from your budget backpacker $1 cup noodle soups, head to Domino's Pizza on their $5 evenings. The second tip is to visit **Peterpan's Travel** agency. They have offices in every major city and offer good deals for backpackers. On top of that, they have regular party nights on which they offer many free goodies and you get to meet many nice people.

2.3.1 How to pack for long-term travel

In the **free packing list** you get along with this book, everything you need for your time in Australia is listed. It starts with an international charger, goes over socks and ends at camping equipment. However, from the quantity, I can tell you that less is better. You want to be comfortable when going from place to place and every extra kilo will be a nuisance. On top of that, if you sleep at hostels or on a woofing farm, you will be sharing your room with many other travelers who are in the same situation as you. You will be glad if your luggage doesn't need much space and perhaps fits into the locker in the room. From my experience, I can pack about the same things whether I go travel for three weeks or half a year. You have to consider whether you need winter and summer clothes but other than that, just bring clothes for about three weeks of not washing. The latest at every three weeks you'll just have to wash your things.

2.3.2 Which Australian sim card should you buy?

There are three main mobile networks to choose from, operated by **Telstra, Optus,** and **Vodafone**. All are GSM networks, offering 4G services. This means that visitors from most of Europe and Asia will be able to use an Australian SIM card in a phone they already own.

Apart from those three, there are many smaller providers. These companies sell services from either Telstra, Optus or Vodafone but often get you more for your money.

Of the three networks, it's said that Telstra has the best coverage, especially in rural areas. However, even with Telstra, I had several days in WA and the NT where I didn't have any reception at all. At first, it was a bit scary for me, then it was liberating. How nice to be away from having to stay connected all the time and just enjoy the moment you are in.

You can buy a sim card and an internet plan as soon as you land at the airport in Australia or at convenience stores like 7/11, Coles and Woolworths or the phone stores directly.

2.3.3 How to find work on a work and travel visa

Like for travel partners, cars, and camping utensils, you can find work on **www.gumtree.com.au/**.

My dream job would have been to work at a Peterpan's Travel Agency (lots of young people work there) or at a hostel. It doesn't hurt to ask and so, simply write them an e-mail with your application papers. Unfortunately, I'm not eligible for work and travel as a Swiss person. However, I still wanted to have this experience and luckily, my flatmate in Melbourne was the manager of a restaurant. So, I could distribute flyers for the restaurant and work at the bar for cash. This was a fun experience and the team was nice so that I made some local Australian friends.

However, the typical job for people on a working holiday visa is **farm work**.
There are plenty of jobs available and you will **find a job just by asking people** once you are in Australia. Therefore, I don't see the need for buying one of the many "welcome packages" you can buy on the internet. However, if you are very insecure, such a package might be a good option for you. On the other hand, you can also apply for temporary jobs online. I've heard many different stories of people who worked in Australia. In some places, you will have a great experience with awesome people and in other

places, you will have a horrible boss who takes advantage of backpackers. My recommendation is: don't do this to yourself. If you don't like the atmosphere in one place, don't waste time by staying there. There will be a much nicer place to work in another city. Australia is a big and beautiful country after all.

The following websites let you know about plenty of jobs.

http://www.backpackerjobboard.com.au/

http://ibackpacker.com.au/

https://www.seek.com.au/backpacker-jobs

Make sure when you apply for the job, to let your employer know that you are on a working holiday visa and provide them with the necessary documentation for them to hire you. Remember, if you do 88 days of farm work you will be entitled to apply for a **second-year visa** in Australia.

Tip: Don't forget to hand in your tax form until 30. June for all the work you did before that. Your employer or co-workers can help you with that. As a non-resident, you will get the 32.5% taxes you paid refunded. However, only if you hand in the tax form on time.

Wwoofing

Wwoof is an organization which offers **worldwide opportunities on organic farms**. You will work from 5-7 hours each day and receive food and accommodation in return. With wwoofing as well you can land on an awesome farm or on a farm which isn't applying wwoof in its true spirit. Best check out their website (https://wwoof.com.au/) to see if this is something you'd like to do. It costs $70 per year to sign up as a backpacker.

2.3.4 How to open up a bank account in Australia and get a social security number

If you want to work in Australia, you probably also would like to get paid. It's very easy to open up a bank account in Australia as a foreigner. They are used to work and travelers and will know what you talk about once you show up at a bank.
I can recommend **National Bank Australia (NAB)** as it's free to open up an account and handling the account will be free for the first two years. Other banks have fees for that. You could compare some more banks online of course.
Then, you go to the bank of your choice after arriving in Australia and bring **your passport with the visa** and an **Australian address** (for example from the hostel). Perhaps it's also good to be able to use google translate as you have to fill out some forms and might not understand all the terms on it.

After you signed all the papers, you will receive some forms which you need to keep safe with you. Your bank card will be sent to the address which you told them within a week. In case you might not be at that hostel anymore you could also tell them to send the bank card to a bank building directly. Then, you can get it there once it arrives. This might be a good idea either way because the post service at a hostel might not be 100% reliable.

The Tax File Number

With every new job, you must tell your employer your tax file number (TFN) along with some other data. This is very important in order to save money from the tax authorities. With the TFN the tax for work and travelers are 32.5 %. Without it, it's 48.5%. So, it's worth it to get the TFN soon after arriving in Australia. You can only get it after your arrival though, as your name needs to be registered with the authorities. To receive the Australian tax file number (TFN) you have to go online (www.ato.gov.au/individuals/tax-file-number/apply-for-a-tfn/foreign-passport-holders,-permanent-migrants-and-temporary-visitors---tfn-application/) and fill out the forms. This takes 15-20 minutes. You need your **passport information** and an **Australian address**. After completing the form, it will take two to four weeks until you receive your TFN delivered to the address you told them. If you need it before that, you can call the government (+61 13 2861) and ask whether you can already know your TFN.

2.3.5 How to spend your nights in Australia

In Australia, you have the choice to sleep in a swag (Australian one-person tent) below the stars, take a camper van, go couch surfing, woofing, rent a holiday home or stay at any accommodation ranging from low budget hostel to luxury resort.
Following, I listed some pros and cons for each type of accommodation and how to best find that kind of accommodation.

Hostel or Hotel

Australia's hostel and hotels have a good standard, however. Therefore, an average night at a hostel costs $25. A bit pricier than in Asia. I recommend booking a night through **booking.com** since they have good deals and you can read the real reviews of travelers like me. The plus of a hostel is that you can come and go as you please and there most likely is an equipped kitchen, where you can cook and therefore keep up your budget backpacker life. The big negative point of Australian hotels is that, especially along the East coast, many groups partied in their room and drank alcohol although that was prohibited. It's not agreeable if you later want to sleep in that room. Secondly, I had never suffered from other people having sex in my dorm until I came to Australia. There, it happened all the time. Seriously, get more creative, people. If you travel along the East coast in hostels, it will be a wonder if that doesn't happen to you. Hence, the big plus of a hotel; you will have peace and quiet. On the other hand, it will be harder to meet other people and make friends in hotels and there probably won't be a kitchen. However, who cares, if you are not on a budget. Restaurants in Australia are first class.

Couchsurfing

For Couchsurfing, you have to be registered on their platform (www.couchsurfing.com/) and plan ahead. You need to contact possible hosts which takes a lot of time. Then, hosts probably expect you to spend time with them since after all, Couchsurfing is to share cultures and stories. So, Couchsurfing takes a bit of work to find a good host and you won't be entirely independent, but you can meet awesome people and feel like a local. I always feel more at home in a country when I am staying with a nice Couchsurfer. Plus, you get to spend the night for free and can save money.

Woofing

As explained in the "How to find a job" section, with wwoof (https://wwoof.com.au/) you will work for 5-7 hours per day and receive accommodation and food in return. This only is the right option for you, if you want to stay longer in one place. Since this is usually on a farm, it will most likely be a rural place in the outback without much going on. If this is, what you wish for your time in Australia to be like, wwoofing is perfect for you.

Camping

By camping, I mean sleeping in a tent, an RV, a van or a car. The main thing is that you can cater for yourself for a few nights. Australia probably is one of the most wonderful countries to be able to spend a night somewhere in nature, below the stars. In Australia, you can still be hundreds of kilometers away from the next people. This makes you notice nature more intensely. You hear the sounds better and really have the time to take in your surroundings. This complete freedom you only have when you go camping. The downside is when the weather doesn't play along. You might be freezing in some nights, too hot in others and curse the rain when everything is soaked once more. Plus, it's quite a lot of work to set up all the utensils for cooking and sleeping and putting them away every day again, when you move on to a different spot. Yet, I had some of the best nights of sleep in the Australian outback with such clean air.

A must-have app when you are doing road trips in Australia is Wiki Camps Australia (https://play.google.com/store/apps/details?id=au.com.angryrobot.wikicamps&hl=en). It shows you anything from where the campsites are, how much they cost (whether they are free), what facilities there are and what route best to take to drive there.

> **Tip**: Probably you have a cooler in your equipment to cool meat or other food. Instead of always buying ice, you could spend nights at campsites which have a freezer in the public kitchen and then you can freeze plastic water bottles to take with you the following day.

In case you are ever going camping with Australian's they will most likely want to impress you by pointing out the Southern Cross (Australia's most famous star formation which even made it onto their flag) to you. Surprise them by already knowing where it is because you looked it up on the internet.

2.3.6 Buying a car vs. traveling with other people who have a car vs. renting a car and public transport

Again, all those options have advantages and disadvantages and therefore we look at each of them uniquely.

Buying a car

First things first, whatever you are looking for in Australia you will find it on https://www.gumtree.com.au/. Whether it is a car, a travel partner, a couch, old CDs, they sell or give away anything on Gumtree. I found my car there, and I found three travel partners, plus, I sold my camping gear again through Gumtree in the end.

So, the difficult thing about buying a car is finding one that suits your needs and fits your budget. If you buy a cheap car, you might have to pay a lot to fix it. It's important that the car is reliable out in the outback. Unfortunately, I was a bit of a dumb blonde when I bought my Toyota Corolla wagon, which looked so cool because it came with a surfboard on the roof and a lot of camping gear. I haggled the price down to $1000, paid $850 more to get it ready for the road again and then it broke down after 1.5 months of driving it only. Hm, perhaps I shouldn't have taken a car with over 300000 km on it already. Luckily, I could sell the car to a scrap yard and the camping gear to another traveler and made back $450. So, it probably still came cheaper than renting a car and it was a great feeling to have my own car and the freedom of driving anywhere I wanted.

Having a car is a must on the West Coast and South Coast, and if you aren't doing any group tours, also the NT. At the North East Coast, it's nice to have. However, along the East Coast, you don't really want to have a car as parking spots in the cities are limited and expensive.

One more thing you must pay attention to when buying a car is where the license of the car you buy is registered. In Australia, it's mandatory that you register the car with your name as soon as you purchase it and that must be done in the same state as where the license is registered. You don't want to buy a car in Perth which you have to register in Victoria.

Traveling with other people who have a car

Here, the good thing is that you don't have any risks about the car but on the other hand you have to find someone who is driving the route you want or perhaps you have to adjust your plans a little.

Renting a car

Renting a car is convenient because you can decide you want to drive somewhere and then rent a car the same day and leave. The two previous choices take a bit more planning. However, renting a car in Australia is expensive. Check for rates online. There are the usual rental companies like Budget, Avis or Sixt. If you want to hire a van, Wicked Campers (www.wickedcampers.com.au/) are famous in Australia.

Public transportation

In the big cities, there's always a bus or tram you can take to all the important stops and you don't need a car. Between cities, it might be a bit more difficult, except for the East Coast, where Greyhound (www.greyhound.com.au/) is bringing you everywhere. You can even buy hop on hop off passes, which make the legs cheaper. The downside is that travel with public transportation will slow you down because you have to adjust to a schedule. Sometimes, they are late. On the other hand, some Greyhound buses had WIFI and USB-chargers and it's comfortable if you can simply hang back while being transported.

2.4 Driving on the other side of the road

Surprisingly, I got used to driving on the other side of the road very quickly. It's easy to drive anyway on such long, empty, straight roads. A dream actually. It will be very odd when you suddenly arrive at a stop light after having driven over 300 km without having had to stop once due to traffic.

The only thing that caused a few laughs was that the handlebar for the blinkers and the windshield wipers are on reversed sides. So, sometimes when making a turn, I accidentally put on the windshield wipers :) I saw other people doing it as well. It's just something you do automatically.

2.5 How to navigate in Australia

All the roads are well signposted, and you'll find the places you need. However, to have the big overview it's best to have some good maps on your phone. I used **Wiki Camps Australia** (https://play.google.com/store/apps/details?id=au.coc.angryrobot.wikicamps&hl=en) and like in all the other countries I travel to, **maps.me** (https://maps.me/). You find them both in your phone's store for free. With those two maps, you can't get lost, as long as your phone has power. Hence, bring actual power banks or a charger for the car.

3 Travel routes for two to three weeks of vacations

3.1 Three-week itinerary for Australia's West-Coast, the North and the Red Center

The wild and beautiful west of Australia is worth exploring by travelers who love adventure. You won't be able to close your mouth because of all the marvelous things you will see. The only thing you can't underestimate is the big distances you have to cover in your car. But don't worry, on Australia's straight and empty roads, driving is not as annoying as in Europe. You won't get stuck in a single traffic jam and covering over 2000 km in two weeks will give you a feeling of freedom as you have never experienced it before.

Day 1: Arrival in Perth

Take a stroll through the **CBD**, get accustomed to the warm climate. For lunch, enjoy a meal at **Annalakshmt**, an Indian vegan restaurant, where you pay as much as you'd like. In the afternoon, enjoy a swim at **Cottesloe** or **Scarborough Beach** where you can also stay to watch the sunset. Another option would be to head to **Kings Park** in the late afternoon and take a walk through the beautiful garden. You have a great view over Perth and it's also a nice place to see the sunset and then observe how the city lights shine in the evening sky.

If you aren't tired yet, go out in **Northbridge**. There are many cool bars and there is some kind of special at a different pub or club every night.

Day 2: Perth

In the morning, you take the 20mins drive to **Fremantle** where you can have a delicious cup of coffee. Hopefully, you are there from Friday to Sunday, because then, you can have lunch at the awesome market in Fremantle. Apart from that, there is a nice beach. Of course, you could stay here all afternoon, or you could visit one of the free **art museums** in Perth. For sunset, head to **Herrison Island**. It is located below a bridge that leads out of the center of Perth. It's like a free pet zoo for kangaroos. The best chance to see the kangaroos is shortly before sunset because that's when the rangers feed them.

Day 3: Bunbury and Margaret River

Start your day early and drive to the **dolphin discovery center** in Bunbury. Watch the free dolphin feeding and observe how the dolphins are playing around in the water. Then, drive on to Margaret River, to get there by mid-morning. Go to the visitor center and get a map of the area to start your tour of the **wineries, the chocolate, and the cheese factory**. In all the places, they offer free tastings and therefore this will turn into a very enjoyable day. In case you can't see any more food or drinks, drive to the beach which is incredibly beautiful.

Day 4: Pemberton

After gaining the calories from yesterday, you might feel like exercising today and therefore, drive on to Pemberton. There, you find trees with platforms on up to 75 m. Those trees were used by firemen to spot bushfires, now the tourists can climb them. Drive on to **Albany** for the evening to enjoy this backpacker-friendly town.

Day 5: Wave Rock

In the morning, you could visit **Porongroup National Park** and do the hike to **Granite Skywalk**. Then drive on to the famous **Wave Rock** in Hyden. This is a massive rock wall which looks like a wave. After taking a stroll around this awesome place, you can drive the remaining distance back to **Perth**, where you will stay one more night, before starting your drive into the outback tomorrow.

Day 6: Pinnacle Desert

From now on, it would be best to get up with the sun and go to bed with the sun in order to make the most of the day. From now on, we are heading north. Drive to **Nambung NP** where you find a yellow desert with lots of straight pinnacles growing out of the earth. You will drive through this national park by car and stop at different lookout points. After that, drive on to **Kalbarri**, where you can already visit the two lookout points at the impressive cliffs and then take a swim in the bay.

Day 7: Kalbarri

Get up early in the morning and visit the highlights of Kalbarri NP while it isn't yet so hot. The best picture opportunity is **Nature's Window**. The destination for the night will be **Coral Bay**. This is a paradise beach with a small reef to snorkel. It's a seven-hour drive north of Kalbarri and therefore, you must calculate some time for the drive but there are neat stops to quickly hop out of the car along the way, too. For example, the famous **Shell Beach**.

Day 8: Coral Bay to Karijini

Relax at the beautiful Coral Bay in the morning and then start your drive away from the coast toward **Karijini NP**. Now, Australia will more and more look like the outback you expected it to. Red, straight roads and the distances between one small town and the next are getting bigger and bigger. **Tom Price** will welcome you with all the convenience you need to prepare yourselves for three days of self-catered camping in wonderful Karijini National Park.

Day 9: Karijini National Park

This incredible national park is incomparable to anything else you have seen before and a highlight of Western Australia. Drive to **Weano Gorge.** It's a bumpy drive but worth it if you like rock climbing. Choose any of the trails there, for example, **Hancock Gorge Trail**. It starts out easy with a latter and a rocky path through the gorge. Then, you'll have to wade through knee-deep water for a section and in the third section, you need to climb between the two narrow rock walls. In the end, you reach **Kermit's pool**, where you can take a bath.
After the gorge, you can enjoy the heat at the top again and drive to **Joffre Gorge** parking lot. From there, it's only a short walk to the lookout point with view on a high waterfall.

Day 10: Karijini NP

After a night out in the beautiful outback, drive to **Fortescue Waterfall** parking lot and then hike down to its pool. The scenery is stunning; red rocks filled with green nature, gorges next to fields and colorful hills. So different from all the dry areas and the coast that you saw up to now. You can swim in this pool or you can continue to **Fern Pool** which is like a free outdoor spa with small fish which will eat the dead skin off your feet. In the beginning of the afternoon, start the drive (about 5.5 hours) to **Port Hedland**, where you will spend the night back at the coast.

In case you don't want to drive all the way to the Northern Territory, you can now also start your **2-day return drive to Perth** and then fly to any other destination in Australia from there.

Day 11: Broome

Today, you have another 6-hour drive in front of you to get to Broome. Start early in the morning, so that you get to Broome for a late lunch. If you arrive at a weekend, you can check out the **Courthouse Markets**. If not, visit the well-preserved **dinosaur footprint** near Gantheaume Point. In case you are in Broome between May and October, you can go for a swim at famous and miles long **Cable Beach**. A must throughout any time of the year is to watch the amazing sunset at the beach and perhaps take a camel ride. Tonight, you could go for Asian food, since Broome has one of the biggest Asian communities outside of China and Japan.

Day 12: Gibb River Road: Windjana Gorge

From April to October, you have the awesome opportunity to drive Gibb River Road with a 4WD and enjoy one of the drives in Australia which are still quite an adventure. If you are there from November to March however, your only driving option to get to the NT is the two-day drive from Broome to Kathrine on the Great Northern Hwy. That one isn't very spectacular and therefore we concentrate on **The**

Gibb. Start early in Broome and drive to **Windjana Gorge National Park.** This is one of the best places in Australia to see freshwater crocodiles in the wild. Take the **Gorge Walk**, which begins at the camping area and winds through the gorge for 3.5 km each way. Spend the night at the self-catered campsite.

Day 13: Gibb River Road: Bell Gorge

Have another early start to get to picturesque **Bell Gorge.**

Bell Gorge is very picturesque and therefore one of the most popular gorges along Gibb River Road. Visit the waterfall which drops 150 meters into a deep pool surrounded by ledges and sheltered by rocky walls. It is a great place for swimming. Drive on to **Galvans Gorge** which is the most accessible gorge along Gibb River Road and a fun one to take a dip.

Day 14: Gibb River Road: Drysdale Homestead

This will be a day of driving in the stunning scenery. At Drysdale Homestead, you can get meals, fuel, ice, and basic supplies. After that, you need to be self-sufficient again.

Day 15: Mitchel Falls National Park

This is one of the most amazing waterfalls in Australia and therefore worth the adventurous drive past King

Edward River Crossing. Once you arrive at **Mitchell Falls Camping** area, choose a spot for the night but then embark on a stunning hike up to Mitchel Plateau, taking swims at all the different natural bathtubs you find along the way. In case you don't want to walk back, you can book a helicopter ride. The pilot will collect you at the top of Mitchel Falls in the afternoon.

Day 16: Gibb River Road

Today you return to Gibb River Road and drive the last stretch to **Kununurra**. It's a hip small town with a big supermarket and the last town in Western Australia. Tomorrow you will enter the Northern Territory.

Day 17: Kathrine

Drive to **Kathrine Gorge** and enjoy your first walk or boat ride in the Northern Territory. After enjoying the scenery of Kathrine Gorge or the **civilization** of the city, drive as close to Litchfield National Park as you can still manage to drive so that you can have a pretty much full day in Litchfield National Park the next day.

Day 18: Litchfield National Park

This is another park for waterfall and bird lovers. Visit **Buley Rockhole** and swim in the natural bathtubs. Afterward, visit both **Florence Falls** and **Wangi**

Falls. Florence Falls are fun to swim in and both waterfalls are incredibly stunning to look at.

Day 19: Mataranka and Devil's Marbles

If you have more time, also visit Kakadu National Park today. If your time is limited, head south again. Once more, you will pass Kathrine, but our first goal of the day is **Mataranka** with its natural hot springs. A nice place to stay an hour or two and soak in the hot water.
Then, drive south through the red and dry outback. Enjoy the magnificent scenery that moves past your window until you reach the enchanted spot of **Devil's Marbles**. Enjoy a walk among the big rocks looking like giant Easter eggs.

Day 20: Uluru

Start early to drive down to **Alice Springs** and take a picture of the big sign that you have arrived at the red center of Australia. You have come a far way but there is one more highlight waiting for you. Continue inland until you reach **Yulara**. Take a sunset camel ride or just enjoy the setting sun behind Australia's most famous rock, Uluru, with a drink in your hand.

Day 21: Uluru

Take a walk around the base of **Ayers Rock** and inform yourself about the culture of Aborigines in the visitor center. Then, drive back to Alice Springs, where you can return your rental car and then take an evening flight to a bigger airport. Or travel on, East or South to reach Sydney or Melbourne by car.

Three weeks is a bit rushed for this big trip and all by car, so if you could make it into four weeks, that would be perfect. Or, skip a few places and fly.

3.2 Three-week itinerary for Australia's East-Coast and Great Ocean Road

The East coast is the more popular route to travel in Australia. If you travel between Sydney and Cairns you will follow the backpacker trail, as they named it, since most people stop in the same places. Nevertheless, there are places worth putting onto your travel bucket list. Here is an itinerary to see the best things along the East coast in three weeks.

Day 1: Melbourne

Land in the city which is Australian's favorite city of many Europeans. Enjoy the modern architecture, take a stroll through **Victoria Market**, relax on the **Circle Tram** and listen to the stories about Melbourne and have your first, very delicious and beautifully crafted Australian coffee.

Day 2: Great Ocean Road

With your car, head to **Geelong** and stretch your legs in that cute seaside town before continuing to the start of the Great Ocean Road. You can choose to visit more seaside towns like **Torquay** and famous surf location **Bells Beach** or you can cut through the countryside until you reach **Twelve Apostles** Visitor Facility. Take some pictures of the famous rock formation in the ocean which is also on the front cover of this travel guide. After that, walk down

Gibson Steps and be impressed by the big cliffs. You can spend the night in **Port Campbell**.

Day 3: Great Ocean Road

Drive past the Twelve Apostles again and then continue along the whole Great Ocean Road. You can stop to walk to some waterfalls, search for **koalas** on the drive to Cape Otway or visit a lighthouse. Be sure to time your drive back to Melbourne that you can be in St. Kilda shortly before sunset the latest. In that case, you can watch the small **penguin parade** at the pier in St. Kilda.

Day 4: Canberra

Today, you either fly from Melbourne to Sydney and enjoy a city day in either city, or you drive from Melbourne to Canberra. Visit the **Australian War Memorial** in the capital of Australia. Either, spend the night in Canberra or drive on toward **Blue Mountains National Park**.

Day 5: Blue Mountains

Drive to **Echo Point** and marvel at the famous **Three Sisters**. The view into the huge gorge and valley is impressive and demands to be explored. Hike down **Giant Stairway** and then continue to **Lorne** to return on the **Cliffwalk**.

Day 6: Blue Mountains

Today, do the hike called **National Pass**. It's a fun walk because you will walk along the carved-out mountain and see many beautiful waterfalls (for example **Wentworth Falls**). Then, drive on to Sydney, where you can enjoy a sunset in the harbor area with view of the opera house. You could return your rental car now and take Greyhound bus from now on, or you can simply continue driving on your own.

Day 7: Sydney

In the morning, take a bus to **Bondi Beach** and either take a swim at this famous beach or even the **Iceberg pools**. Or set off for the beautiful **Bondi to Coogee walk.** Later, return to the city and have a bite to eat at the well-known **Sydney Fish Market.** Marvel again at the beautiful bay and the **opera house.** Then, it's time to have a look at Sydney's city life. Look at the shops in **Georg St.** and have a drink in **The Rocks** district.

Day 8: Drive to Byron Bay

Drive north along the coast and stop in all the towns you feel like. For example, you could take some pictures in front of the **Big Banana** in **Coffs Harbor** and sample some freshly made candy.

Day 9: Byron Bay

Enjoy a beach day at the paradise-like beach or walk up to the lighthouse. Up there, you are at the **most Eastern point of Australia** and might spot dolphins and turtles in the water below you. In the evening, enjoy the good vibes of the many bars and pubs in Byron Bay.

Day 10: Brisbane

After closing the short distance between Byron Bay and Brisbane you should take a walk along the river and then hop on a free red **City Hopper ferry.** In **Southbank**, you can relax at the artificial beach and enjoy the atmosphere in the small rainforest. In case you brought nice clothes, you should go out to the club **Cloudland** in the evening. However, all the bars in Brisbane were fun and most of them had live music.

Day 11: Noosa

Drive to Noosa, the beautiful beach town with mangroves and rainforest. Book your canoeing tour for tomorrow.
You could spend a day surfing at the beach or take any of the various nature walks. On Wednesday, I recommend driving to **Eumundi Markets.** They have good deals and you get to sample a lot of the delicious food. For sunset, head up the steep path in Noosa and marvel at the wonderful view in the softening light.

Day 12: Noosa – Mangroves Canoeing Tour

Today, you will be picked up for your **canoeing tour** through the serene mangroves. In a boat, you will be brought up a big stream, past the island from Richard Branson. Afterward, you get to paddle on a smaller creek. Enjoy the jungle like scenery while paddling to your lunch destination. The whole day you will be looked after very well food and drink wise. After lunch, you will paddle back to the starting point and then take the boat back to the jetty.

You should then drive on to **Rainbow Beach**, the hub for tours to Fraser Island which will start tomorrow. Tours to Fraser need to be pre-booked some days or even weeks in advance. You find many different tour options online, from 1-day to 3-day tours.

Day 13: Fraser Island

Whatever option you decide, the tour should include the following highlights:

- Lake McKenzie
- Seventy-Five Mile
- Eli Creek
- Maheno Shipwreck
- Indian Head
- The Champagne Pools
- Lake Wabby

I did a 3-day tour with Cool Dingo but couldn't compare any prices because Peterpan's Travel Agency booked it for me. Cool Dingo is above all for young and active people. However, there are so many tour options, it's best to check them out online yourself beforehand.

Day 14: Fraser Island

Touring Fraser is expensive anyway and in order not to be rushed, you should at least do a 2-day/1-night tour. Enjoy 4WD on the sand and visiting the beautiful freshwater lakes and streams on this island.

Day 15: Driving North

Today, you have a long day of driving ahead of you. Therefore, start early and take enough stops along the way. You should reach **Airlie Beach** in the early evening. Have a swim and a BBQ in the lagoon. Again, you should have pre-booked your two-day one-night tour to the Whitsundays (or whatever length you prefer) beforehand.

Day 16: Whitsunday Cruise

At **Airlie Beach Port** you will board your boat to sail to the Whitsundays. The highlight will be vast and white **Whitehaven Beach**. Be sure to walk to the lookout point. That is the most spectacular view along the East coast of Australia.

Day 17: Whitsunday Cruise

After a night on the boat with an incredible night sky full of stars since you are so far away from any lights, you can enjoy another day on sea visiting pretty islands and sandbanks.

Day 18: Drive North

One more driving day to cover some distance and make it to the biggest city in the North-East of Australia; **Cairns**. Stop in as many of the picturesque seaside towns along the way as you'd like.

Day 19: Great Barrier Reef

A day trip to the outer reef of the Great Barrier Reef needs to be pre-booked as well. Enjoy a day on the ocean with nice meals which are prepared by the boat crew. **Snorkel or scuba dive** in the yet very diverse Great Barrier Reef.

Day 20: Waterfalls

Today, you need a car again as you go explore **Tablelands**. This will be a day for waterfall lovers as you will get to see at least six different and picturesque waterfalls. A highlight might be **Millaa Millaa Falls** which are famous from some shampoo commercials.

Day 21: Flight or trip to the Daintree Rainforest?

Today, it's time to fly home or onward. However, if you have another day to spare, hop in your car again and take a day trip into Daintree National Park. You will cross a river on a **car ferry** to get there. Or, just relax in Cairn's lagoon and take a walk along the esplanade.

Hopefully, you have more time in Australia than three weeks and therefore can visit many more highlights. In the following chapters, I will tell you in detail, how to visit all the incredible places Down Under has to offer.

4 Must see stops along the West Coast (WA)

Perth is the closest city to Europe to fly into and therefore it's a bit of a mystery to me, why only such a small amount of people dedicates their attention to the West Coast of Australia. This side of Australia is much more adventurous than the East Coast and the nature you find here isn't comparable to anything else you find on the world. Such stunningly beautiful places shouldn't be missed and therefore a trip up and down WA should be on every road trip lover's bucket list.

> **Tip:** Buy the National Park entrance pass online (https://shop.dbca.wa.gov.au/collections/park-passes) before you go. You can get a Holiday Pass for four weeks at $46 or a yearly pass for $92 (concession rate is $58). The pass is valid for one vehicle. One park usually costs $13 per car and $8 per motorcycle. There also are some offices where you can buy the park pass (for example Perth Visitor Center) but it's not possible to buy the pass at every national park and therefore it's better to get one before you start your trip.

Here are the must-see places in Western Australia.

4.1 Perth

Perth is the capital of Western Australia and most likely the airport you arrive at if you plan on exploring Western Australia.
The city offers nice shops, beautiful parks, a pretty river, and a lovely ocean front. You find good restaurants, beaches to relax at and festivals and museums to make your culture heart beat a little faster. To make your visit to Perth even more agreeable, the CBD is equipped with fast working free Wi-Fi.

4.1.1 How to get from the airport into the city center

Oh, how wonderful it was to escape the Swiss winter and step out of the plane at 35 °C in February. This time, the security measures weren't as strict as the last time (our plane wasn't sprayed with any disinfectant and they didn't look through my suitcase and take anything away from me.) However, I still needed to wait for almost an hour to get my passport stamped. At least afterward, I spotted my backpack on the carousel right away. I made it out of the airport without any further delays.

- The quickest but most expensive way is taxis. For about $45 you get to the city center or for $55 to Scarborough.

- The second option is Perth City Shuttles. Look for CONNECT booths to buy a ticket. A return ticket is $18 for adults and the shuttles will drive you to various points across the city.

- The cheapest way, however, is by Transperth Bus #37 for $4. There is no public bus outside T1 and T2 and therefore you have to take a free transfer bus to the domestic terminal. The bus stop can be found in front of T4. Cross two lanes of traffic and turn right. The stop is marked by a white and green sign. Bus #37 to the city center leaves every 20 to 30 minutes. This is its route: Outside Domestic Terminal T4 - Brearley Ave - Stanton Rd - Johnson St - Belmont - Belmont Forum - Alexander Rd - Belmont Forum/Wright St - Kooyong Rd - Great Eastern Highway - Past Burswood - Victoria Park Transfer Station (30 mins) - City Centre (Adelaide Terrace, St Georges Terrace, Fraser Rd, Kings Park (55 mins) - some buses then continue to the Esplanade Busport and others go to Fraser Av/Kings Park.

From the bus stops, you can interchange to other buses. Just ask the driver or the locals to find the way to your hotel. Australian people are generally very friendly and helpful.

4.1.2 What to do in Perth

Free Walking Tour

Free walking tours are a great and fun way to discover a new city and get a good feel for it. They are led by volunteers who work on tip basis and you donate as much as you want at the end of the tour. In Perth, the starting point is the **iCity Information Kiosk** in the Murray Street Mall at the intersection of Forrest Place. The tour starts every day (except public holidays) at 9.45 a.m. and lasts 90 minutes. Be there at least five minutes before the start.

Take a free CAT bus

Certain buses within the city center, called CAT buses, are free. So, in case your feet are tired, just hop on a free bus for a ride. The other buses you have to pay but if you have a student card you might get a student discount on public transport.

Eat healthily and pay as much as you want

Perth has an awesome restaurant which is located right next to Swan River and the famous Bell Tower. At **Annalakshmt** (Jetty 4 Barrack Square) you can eat on a beautiful terrace. You serve yourself from a vegetarian Indian buffet, water or fruit juice are available as well and at the end, you just donate as much as you want. What a great idea at such a nice location!

Go shopping

- Murray St and Hay St are good for shopping. That's where I bought an Australian sim card for my phone.

- In the Harbor Town shopping center, you can find some good deals because it's full of outlet stores. It's located along the Yellow CAT line.

Stroll through Kings Park

Take the bus to Kings Park which is on a hill just outside the city and on top of it is a beautiful (free) botanical garden. There is an awesome glass bridge, with an even better view over the river and the city of Perth. It's not only a good place during the day but also to watch the sunset and take pictures of the city lights after sunset.

Relax at a beach

- **Cottesloe beach** is the closest beach to the CBD and has a true paradise feel to it. The sand is white and the water very blue. To enter the beach, you walk down a sandy path through a green patch and some people came by bicycle which are parked along the path. → Nice spots for Instagram pictures.

- **Trigg Beach:** Another nice beach where it's possible to surf beginner waves and we even lucked out and saw a small whale quite close to the beach.

- **Scarborough Beach:** This is another famous beach in Perth and good to enjoy a cider at sunset.

Visit a museum (many museums in Perth are free)

- **The Art Gallery**: Apart from being nicely air conditioned it's free and has awesome paintings from Australian artists as well as Picassos and the famous French painters! It's worth the visit if you like art!

Go out in Northbridge

One of the coolest quarters to go out in Perth is Northbridge. There are many cool bars and there is some kind of special at a different pub or club every night. Our favorites were the Thursday specials at **Mustang Bar** (burger for $5) and good music and steak with fries and a drink for $15 at The Court. The Court welcomes gay people. On Thursday, it also is quiz night and your dinner will be quite entertaining.

Observe semi-wild kangaroos on Herrison Island

Herrison Island is located below a bridge that leads out of the center of Perth and is best reached by car. If you arrive with the free city bus, it's a bit far to walk in hot weather. It's like a free pet zoo for kangaroos. The best chance to see the kangaroos is shortly before sunset because that's when the rangers feed them. Once you arrive at the parking lot, walk along the path under welcoming shade from trees. The island with the water around it looks very pretty. It would be awesome to swim here but there are "no swimming" signs and the water is probably not deep and clean enough.

One side of the island is a normal park, where you can walk around. The other side is the same, except that there are semi-wild living kangaroos. We had to enter inside the fenced part through a door you would normally find at a pet zoo. The first kangaroo we spotted came hopping through a forest. It let me come so close that I could pet it. But once it realized that I didn't have any food, it lost interest in me. Afterward, we found a whole group of kangaroos and none of them was scared of us. That was quite a cool experience!

Visit Caversham Wildlife Park

Caversham (www.cavershamwildlife.com.au/plan-your-visit/) is a zoo where some animals are in cages and others roam around freely and therefore you can get very close to the animals. We met the cutest Koala ever (I would have loved to take him home) but otherwise, many of the animals seemed sad because they didn't have enough space to hide from the tourists. For kids, the park and the shows or animal encounters are a nice experience but as an adult, I wouldn't go there again. (Cost for adult: $29)

After about 3h30min, we had seen everything and since it was still early, we drove through the pretty Swan Valley. A must do stop for chocolate lovers is the **Margaret River Chocolate Company.** You can eat free chocolate drop samples and apart from chocolate, you can also taste wine for free at one of the wineries. Swan Valley is not as big as Margaret River but absolutely worth a visit when you want to get away from Perth for an afternoon.

Visit Yanchep National Park

This national park is located 40 driving minutes north of Perth. It's similar to the Everglades in Florida. You can walk over a wooden path except that you won't be looking for alligators but for koala bears instead. Of course, they were all sleeping but it's nice to see koala bears in nature. There also is a swamp that used to be a lake, where we saw a group of kangaroos resting in the shade.

4.2 Fremantle

Freo is a town just south of Perth. From there you can take the ferry to Rottenest Island which is expensive to do but very beautiful. However, Fremantle is a place to fall in love with on its own. You will find a nice beach, one cuter café after the other, loads of nice bars with live music and beautiful houses everywhere.

> **Tip:** From Friday to Sunday there's a big market in a market hall which you shouldn't miss! Be hungry when you go there because they sell so many nice foods and sweets from all over the world (even German Bratwurst) and if you go there around 4 p.m. the fruit section will start reducing the prices. There also is a section with clothes, jewelry, and other nice things.

From the market, you can walk to the beach and will discover a fort. From the top, there is a wonderful view over the ocean and once you walk back down, you will reach a very picturesque harbor.

Apart from the beautiful beachside and the pretty city, there are many places with free Wi-Fi. Another cool thing about Freo is that there are public instruments located all over the city center. They invite people to play the piano or some percussion instruments and the melodies spread a happy feeling around town.

Rottnest Island

From Fremantle, you can take the ferry to the holiday destination Rottnest Island. Visit the cute Quokkas and see them hopping around, enjoy the various beaches, restaurants and water activities. Admission to the island is $18.50 for a day visitor and 24.50 if you stay the night. However, you also have to get there. The ferry ticket starts at $84 for a same day return ticket. Find out about the different ferry options here: www.rottnestisland.com/the-island/getting-here/by-ferry.

4.3 Bunbury

Bunbury is only 90 minutes driving south of Perth and there is a **dolphin discovery center**, where they do pretty much the same thing as in Monkey Mia. Except that the employees here are more open than in Monkey Mia and the dolphins come very close and even have fun playing around a little in front of the tourists. So, all things considered, I found this experience much better than in Monkey Mia because it's not such a waste of gas money and you won't be harming the nature by driving up there just for dolphins. They don't have a specific feeding time since dolphins are coming and going all day and there will be volunteers at the interaction zone. From October to April you can also book a swim with the dolphins' cruise (http://dolphindiscovery.com.au/enjoy/swim-encounter/).

4.4 Busselton

In Busselton, you find a 1,8 km long jetty. A train can bring you to the end and back, but you could also just pay $2.50 to walk across it and enjoy a walk over the ocean. However, it's also nice to take a walk along the beach and take pictures of the jetty from ashore.

4.5 Margaret River

This was one of my favorite regions in Australia. It's a place for foodies and the main thing you do here is touring the different wineries and food factories and sample all their delicacies for free. Stop at the **visitor center**, where they have free WIFI and will give you a map with all the **wineries**. It's very common to do self-drive tours from winery to winery and therefore it might be that people are a bit tipsy behind the wheel. So, just watch out a little more than usual, while being on the road. We visited one winery in the morning, had lunch and then we visited one winery in the afternoon. In between, we also paid a visit to the cheese and chocolate factory and collected delicious items for our lunch platter. Margaret River is the land of milk and honey and if you only have one day in Margaret River, I'd recommend visiting these places:

The Berry Farm
Vessel
Chocolate Factory
Dairy Factory (Cheese)
Voyager Estate

However, I'd recommend staying for several days and give yourself a little holiday. The coast of Margaret River is also stunningly beautiful. It looks so wild and romantic! Plus, if you are an intermediate surfer, you can enjoy the waves in Margaret River.

4.6 Caves and stingrays

You can take the scenic Caves Rd toward Augusta and visit **Jewel Caves.** If you haven't seen any caves in Asia yet, this will be a nice cave to visit. However, if you already visited some caves, we recommend continuing to **Hamelin Bay**, where you can encounter big stingrays. They swim up to the beach and take a sunbath. If you are lucky, you find some fishermen who will give you a fish to feed to them.

At **Cape Augusta,** you will find a picturesque lighthouse. On top of that, this is the cape where the Indian Ocean meets the Southern Ocean. I was convinced one side looked greener than the other :)

4.7 Pemberton fire lookout trees

Pemberton is above all known for its tall Karri trees which were used by firemen to spot fires. Now, they are an amazing tourist spot as you won't find it anywhere else in the world. If you like climbing or rope adventure parks you will love the trees in Pemberton!

Warren National Park

At a 15-minutes-drive from Pemberton, you find **Bicentennial Tree**. This is a 75 m (!) high tree which the fireman used to climb on top of to watch out for fires. Now it's open for tourists to climb. I couldn't believe that you can do this without any safety lines or without a ranger watching over the tree. We were the only ones at the tree! It should be quite safe because there are steel poles every 20 cm hammered inside the tree trunk, forming a ladder that leads around the tree and on the side is something like a safety net. So, only if you lose your strength and fall in between the poles because you slip or pass out it would become problematic. Here, you kind of saw the ground constantly whenever you reached for one of the thin poles! So, for the first 20 m, vertigo was quite bad, but nevertheless, I climbed on to at least make it to the first platform. Finally there, I hugged the tree to calm my nerves and pretend that we were on something solid which wasn't moving in the wind. My friend was so motivated to reach the top, that I climbed on too and it got easier after a while. In the end, it was just steel ladders from platform to platform. From the top, there was an enormous view over the Karri forest as far as the ocean.

Unfortunately, there is no lift or zip line, so everything you climbed up, you have to go down again. At least, the ground came closer with every pole you step down. On the ground again, you will feel proud that you just climbed 75 m without being attached to a rope.

Gloucester National Park

Gloucester Tree is the second highest tree (61 m) you can climb, and we also checked this one out. There was one person at the top and another couple climbing it. Somebody was waiting on the benches on the safe ground. It probably was too high for him to climb. I didn't blame him because here, the first platform is on about 40 m and there's no break before that. Yet, it's a fun achievement as well.

4.8 Denmark

In this town, you can find more wineries to go wine tasting, a cheese factory, and a chocolate company. In case your desire isn't satisfied from Margaret River yet, you can immerse yourself in tasting again here. **Green Pool** is a beautiful bay for a lunch stop to enjoy the nice ocean view.

4.9 Albany

Albany is a very backpacker friendly town. There are a few free campsites close to town, there are free hot showers and toilets close to the visitor center and everything should be drinking water if it's not indicated differently. The Wi-Fi at the library is free, too. In addition, the lady at the visitor center is very friendly and will give you a helpful map of the area.

The Gap and Natural Bridge

This is a small gorge in the ocean that the waves fill up and empty out again and again. Right close by is a rock formation that looks like a bridge. It's huge and the people walking around on it look tiny.

Blowholes

In Torndirrup National Park right close to The Gap and Natural Bridge there is a 30 mins walk to some gaps in the rock through which the ocean sometimes pushes water up high in the air. Unfortunately, this natural spectacle doesn't happen every day, and in order not to walk down there in vain, you could ask other tourists in the park who have already done the walk, if the blowholes are actually blowing. In addition, walking around the blowholes on a windy day is dangerous because the rock is rather exposed. Yet, the rumbling of the water below does sound impressive and scary.

4.10 Porongroup National Park

The highlight here is **Granite Skywalk**. A cool metal construction around the top of the rock. To get there, park the car at **Castle Rock** car park. The track to get there is a 2,2 km long walk. For the first 50 mins, it's a steady uphill path that anyone could walk. Then, you reach some fantastic looking rocks. One of them is called **Balancing Rock**. It is set on top of another one, like a sculpture. After 50 m more you reach a lookout from which you have a great view across the countryside. We probably would have seen the ocean if the weather was better. After that, it's just a short climb to **Granite Skywalk** which is a fun steel platform. It's a cool hike but way more touristic than the hikes in Karijini.

4.11 Wave Rock

This is a massive natural rock wave and with that definitely a unique site which should be visited! It's located in Hyden, which is 350 km north of Albany (inland) and therefore a bit out of the way but worth a detour on your route back to Perth.

At the beginning of the walk toward Wave Rock, there is a machine where you must buy a $10 parking ticket for the car. If you are lucky, the people before you will even pass their ticket on to you (or you to the next people). However, it's a nice souvenir as well.

The walk along the huge wave and back on top of it takes about one hour if you take it slow. It's incredible how slippery the rock is if you try to pose for a surfing picture but a fun thing to do either way.

4.12 Lucky Bay in Cape Le Grand National Park

In Cape Le Grand NP you can find some of the most beautiful beaches of Australia. **Hellfire Bay** is a sight for sore eyes with white sand and different shades of blue water. It's very inviting to swim and, luckily, safe as well. Our favorite was **Lucky Bay**. This bay already looks amazing when you drive toward it. There, you really see the contrast of the clear blue water next to the white sand and the green bushes. Since the bay is so big, you can walk along the sand until you are completely alone (same in Hellfire Bay, we were the only people). However, the most amazing thing about Lucky Bay is, that there are kangaroos on the beach! And at the campground too.

From Esperance, you can drive on to **Norseman** from where you'll start the great drive across the Nullarbor Plain in order to reach **Adelaide** in Victoria. That's a road not many tourists take but if your goal is to drive once around Australia, you will have to take this 1000 km straight road. Or, you can drive back to Perth with a detour to **Wave Rock**.

4.13 Nambung National Park (Pinnacle Desert)

Up to now, the route has led from Perth all the way down south. Now we are back in Perth and will explore the north.

Take Indian Ocean Dr. to head north from Perth. You will see a mixture of red-brown dirt with green bushes, trees, and sometimes yellow fields until you arrive at Nambung National Park. This one shouldn't be missed.
Nambung National Park was our first national park and, unfortunately, I did not previously buy the national park pass. So, I had to pay the entrance fee, but the lady gave us a form with which we could get a refund for our money once we'd buy the WA holiday pass.

If you already have your national park pass visible below your windshield you are free to start Pinnacle Drive, which was a yellow sand road that led through hundreds of yellow rocks which were scattered all over the place. It reminded me a bit of a cemetery except that the feeling was completely different in that warm light and these surroundings.

You can get out of the car at places where you can pull the car over and take pictures with the yellow pinnacles. We saw only one other van while we were on the drive and being so alone there was quite cool.

> **Tip:** The next bigger town up north is Geraldton. It's good for shopping last-minute things you forgot to pack in Perth. Enjoy the a/c in the shopping center and Target's free Wi-Fi.

4.14 Kalbarri National Park

Before you reach the town of Kalbarri, take a small detour to **Natures Window Lookout**. It's a beautiful lookout point over cliffs and the waves of the Indian Ocean. If you have time, also drive to the lookout point before that to have a view on the stunning cliffs from the other side as well.

> **Tip:** Buy a fly protection hat (a hat with a net) and bring it on this trip. The flies in Kalbarri and some other places in WA and the center of Australia are more annoying than anywhere else in the world. They will crawl into your eyes, your nose, and your mouth and without a fly net or a scarf you won't know how to breathe, look or talk. Trust me. You won't believe it before you have experienced this but suddenly you will feel very bad for cows and horses which have to experience this on a daily basis.

To relax after a long day of driving you can enjoy a well-deserved bath in the shallow and calm bay.
For more action head to **Blue Holes**. It is a nice spot 1 km south of Kalbarri, where a reef is protecting smaller reefs from the waves and therefore it's perfect for snorkeling. Another option would be **Red Bluff Beach** where you can enjoy the pretty rock formations there. However, if the waves are too choppy here, better drive back into town and swim at the beach there.

Kalbarri National Park

The entrance to Kalbarri national park is over 10 km out of town and to get to the first lookout point across the gorge it's another 30 km on a very bumpy road. Just bear that in mind and fuel up your car before starting your explorations in this national park.
The highlight in Kalbarri NP is **Nature's Window**. The path from the parking lot to Nature's Window is

500m, which means 1 km to go there and come back. You probably think, pha, that's nothing. Then try walking in this heat… It usually is extremely hot in Kalbarri and therefore you will encounter many signs about the danger of exercising in the heat. For us, the way down to the window was okay but to come back up, even our well-trained hearts were beating quite fast and we first needed a rest at the hut next to the parking lot. That being said, the orange rocks which build Nature's Window and the amazing view over the gorge with the blue river are well worth a visit and you will be able to take many beautiful pictures and pretend to be rock climbers.

Pelican Feeding

Almost every day of the year you can encounter a feeding of the birds with their big beak. It takes place on the Kalbarri shore opposite of Murchison Caravan Park at 8.45 a.m. By the way, Murchinson Caravan Park also is a good place to stay with a freezer in the kitchen and electricity. On the day we watched the feeding, there was a group of about twelve tourists and five pelicans were carefully approaching to receive some fish. A lady explained a few things about the animal and then she threw the first fish into one of their mouths. The rest of the fish, the tourists could throw to them. Afterward, we watched how they walked or flew back to the water and watched them swim around for a while. A donation of one dollar per person is appreciated to cover the cost of the fish and the time of the volunteers.

4.15 Hamelin Pools

The Hamelin Pools are located along West Australia's Coral Coast. Coral Coast sounds nice on its own and therefore shouldn't be skipped. The Hamelin Pool stromatolites are the oldest and largest living fossils on earth. They are part of the Earth's evolutionary history and therefore considered 'living fossils'. To geologists and botanists, Hamelin Pool is a place of great interest. To all the other visitors, it's a place with a nice jetty which leads over these weird rocks in the beautiful turquoise water. Definitely a nice place to take a walk after a long drive. It would be a nice stop to walk around a little after a long drive.

4.16 Shell Beach

Shell Beach is located in the Shark Bay World Heritage Area, 45 km south-east of Denham and close to Hamelin Pools. As the name says it's a beach which consists entirely of small, white shells. The water is such an intense clear blue, which makes it really inviting for swimming.

4.17 Monkey Mia

Monkey Mia is famous for the dolphin encounters and just for that, many tourists take the detour of 170 km (one way) upon themselves just to see how they are being fed. After also having been to Bunbury, I'd recommend skipping Monkey Mia. However, it's still a nice resort with rooms, cabins, dorms, a pool, two restaurants and a green patch where campers can put up their tents. A good place to have a holiday for a few days. However, before you even pay for your campsite or hotel room you have to pay to enter Monkey Mia Park. Only after you filled out the form and dropped the money into the box you can proceed to the reception.
If you are camping, beware of the emus which are freely walking around on the premises. If you don't

always close all the openings of your car or van, they will steal anything edible out of it. We saw this happen to the guys next to us, so we were extremely careful and therefore the emus with their scary eyes didn't bother us. The showers for the campers were beautiful, the water good, and the kitchen at the dormitory site was nice too.

The next morning, we got up for the dolphin feeding. First, we had to just stand there for about 45 mins and wait until the dolphins were comfortable enough or ready to accept fish from us. Throughout the whole time, a ranger was explaining things about the dolphins. That part was interesting, and it was really nice to watch the dolphins swim up close and then disappear again, but it was quite a long time to stand in the sun without really having eaten breakfast. Then, only three tourists are chosen to feed a fish to the dolphin and the chance that it's you is very slim. Luckily, we befriended one of the rangers on the evening before and so I was one of the happy tourists who could place a fish in a dolphin's mouth.

Most of the tourists just stay one night at the resort and then leave after the dolphin feeding. That was our luck as well because there were hardly any people at the beach after the feeding. After a while, the dolphins came back and swam within close distances to us in the water. The temptation to touch them was big but since the rangers repeatedly told us not to do that because we could transmit diseases, I resisted the urge and was just happy to be so close to them in the water. So, this was quite a cool experience.

4.18 Coral Bay – A beautiful beach place

There are only three places to stay in Coral Bay and not really anything else to see except for the paradise-like beach. The colors of the sand and water are amazing. The first part of the water was so clear and a light blue, that we felt like we were swimming in a pool. Then, when the water gets deeper and when the reef starts, the color changes to a darker blue. You can see some nice and cool looking fish if you go snorkel. The reef with the fish begins after you've walked 10 m into the water.
Luckily, there are some shade stands at the beginning of the sand and so you can spend a relaxing day on the sand.

4.19 Exmouth

Exmouth is the biggest city on the way to Cape Range National Park and the main hub for tours to **Ningaloo Reef** and **Cape Range NP**. Ningaloo Reef is famous for its whale shark encounters from April to July and humpback whales from July to October.

> **Tip:** In case you just want a good place for a swim with some shade to relax on the beach, head to **Bundegi Beach**. You can stay below the jetty which offers shade and you will see fish around the jetty in case you brought your snorkeling gear.

4.20 Cape Range National Park

This was one of the nicest national parks to camp in since it felt wild and there were some curious, cute kangaroos checking us out but there still are enough other campers within eyesight that we weren't scared of being out in the wilderness.

> **Tip:** Get up at sunrise and start your hike early. There hardly is any shade in this national park and anything after 11 a.m. will become hard on your body.

Yardie Creek

A good starting point for a hike is Yardie Creek, about 50 km into the park and the southern-most point which is accessible for 2WD cars. The drive there takes a little longer than on a highway since you should only go 60 km/h because of the kangaroos that might jump on the road. All the road-kills you will have seen by now will be reason enough to stick to this speed limit.
The walk at the beginning was very easy, on a straight path but it was already extremely beautiful having the blue ocean and white sand behind us, and the red soil with a blue creek that flowed into orange, red, white rock walls in front of us. Then, the walk became a hike with loose rocks and ups and downs. Still okay for most people but we were glad there weren't any flies in the early morning hours.

We saw some eagles and other birds that whistled nice songs. They sounded like humans who were whistling. Apart from the animals we also met a guy who told us how he has been traveling for the past two years because he had won the Australian lottery. Lucky him! The view on this hike really is stunning and the drive down to Yardie Creek is worthwhile as well.

Turquoise Bay

Another beautiful beach and a good place to take a dip after a hike. Turquoise Bay is also nice for snorkeling. It is pretty much the same as in Coral Bay though, except that I saw some miniature versions of butterfly fish and other little ones. Perhaps they were babies? Unfortunately, there wasn't any shade. In case you get too hot as well, drive to the visitor center, where they have a great display of information about the park and the animals. Some kangaroos had the same idea as us and were laying in the shade of the center and there are toilets and picnic tables below trees as well.

4.21 Karijini National Park

From Exmouth to **Tom Price**, the main hub for Karijini National Park, it's about a six-hour drive through the Australian outback. Don't let that stop you from visiting Karijini NP. This was my favorite national park ever! Only for this park, a trip to Western Australia is a must for all adventure lovers! We were thrilled about the small town of Tom Price where everything finally was cheaper again. There is a Coles to stock up on groceries and camping utensils before heading into the national park and gas was the cheapest since Perth.

> **Tip:** Before heading into the national park, stop at the tourist information or at a hotel to ask whether it is safe to enter the park. It's possible to get stuck in the park if there are strong rains and the gorges would become dangerous. Therefore, it's safer to visit it only during good weather.

Visitor Center

There is a visitor center inside Karijini National Park as well. You can cool off in their a/c while looking at the displays. It's also a good place to eat your self-made lunch in the shade of the center.

Fortescue Waterfall

You can drive to the parking lot with the same name and then hike down to its pool. The scenery is stunning; red rocks filled with green nature, gorges next to fields that reminded me a bit of Switzerland and colorful hills. So different from all the dry areas and the coast that we had seen until now. And in this mixture of colors, you find a beautiful waterfall with an inviting blue pool. In all the guides it had said that the water was freezing but maybe not in February because it was warmer than the ocean.

Weano Gorge

A bumpy drive to get there but worth it if you like rock climbing a little. The best path at Weano Gorge is **Hancock Gorge trail** that leads to **Kermit's Pool**. Again, the surroundings are just stunning. It starts out easy with a latter and a rocky path through the gorge. Then, you reach a pool with a sign that says you mustn't climb on the rocks. So, time to take your shoes off and roll up your pants because now you need to wade through the water. It was only about 20 cm deep when we were there. When you reach the other side, you are completely surrounded by red walls (they call this place Amphitheater). After that, you are at the start of Spiderwalk. Ugh, yeah, doesn't sound very attractive. I hoped it has its name because you have to climb through the narrow gorge with your hands and feet sticking to both sides and climbing along the gorge wall, and not because there might be spiders hidden in the rocks (I didn't see any). Better hold on to the walls well because there is water below you and perhaps sharp rocks as well. After this short bit, you already reached Kermit's pool, where you can take a bath. The temperature in the gorge is very agreeable compared to the heat at the top.

Joffre Gorge

From this parking lot, it's only a short distance to the lookout. Again, the view over the gorge and the waterfall was very pretty but there wasn't as much water flowing down as at the other waterfalls.

Fortescue Falls and Fern Pool

Apart from simply looking at the pretty waterfall, you should hike a little further to **Fern Pool**. On the walk, you might spot an iguana. Fern pool is very neat and a little bigger than the one at the Fortescue Falls. There also were two small waterfalls at Fern Pool. If you look up, you will see many black spots in the trees. Those aren't rotten fruits but chilling bats which are at least 30 cm long. You can swim in the pool and there might even be some small fish eating your dead skin. Free fish spa :)

4.21.1 Where to continue from here?

It seems like many people skip Karijini, but I would say if you go to WA, that's the place you must see because it's so amazing and different from everything else. In case you drive back down to Perth from here, the first place you can call civilization will be **Newman**. There are many shops, the gas is cheaper and in the visitor center, you can use their strong WIFI.

If you go further south on the Great Northern Hwy you will reach Meekatherra. There aren't many points of interest along the Great Northern Hwy but Meekatherra has to be noted not because it's beautiful but because there is a gold mining super pit. You can see the big gap from the road or by doing one of the walking trails. However, it's not possible to visit it. If you drive this route anyway, it's something interesting to look at just because you won't see such a huge, human-made hole every day. Other than that, Meekatherra is quite creepy as it's somewhat of a ghost town and only Aborigines still living there. It's also known as one of the hottest towns in WA which surpasses the 45 °C several times each December Meekatherra is the Aborigine's word for "little water".

4.21.2 How to deal with road trains

On the Great Northern Hwy, we really got our share of road trains. In Australia, they call big, long trucks road trains. They sometimes were five trucks long or wider than the whole road, so that we had to drive down into the dirt and wait until they crossed us. Unfortunately, there is a bit of a dilemma with overtaking them. They are going pretty fast as well but if the road is broad enough, you can try it. Just be careful with the last wagon as I can start slithering uncontrollably. Also, it would be a problem if the road suddenly got smaller again or if a car is coming from the other side after all. It just takes a while until you finally passed the road train. However, simply not overtaking them isn't really an option because it's very bad for the windshield of your car and if you leave too much space between you and the road train you will soon be sandwiched between two road trains (the one behind you won't keep the necessary breaking distance to you. Don't want to imagine what would happen if the truck in front of you had to do an emergency break…). The coastal highway therefore is more relaxing to drive since there weren't any road trains. On the other hand, it's quite special to see a whole house being transported on a truck.

4.22 Port Headland

If you drive north from **Karijini National Park**, Port Headland will be the first big city you reach and with that, you are back at the coast. The drive from Karijini to Port Headland takes about five and a half hours through the Pilbara region. Port Hedland is a small town with a few larger supermarkets and therefore good to stock up on food and water again. There also are some bars and restaurants. However, apart from a big industrial port, there isn't anything to do for a tourist and so it's just a good place to perhaps spend a night. From here to **Broome** you have another about 610 kilometers of driving ahead of you. A good idea is

to get up early in the mornings and therefore still arriving at your next destination at agreeable times. It's important to take small rests every three hours of driving to keep your energy up!
Between Port Headland and Broome, there isn't much to see other than beaches and dry land. You'll only pass two roadhouses with horrendous prices. Hence, make sure your tank is full and you have enough water and food supplies to cater for yourself.

4.23 Broome

Broome is the hub to start exploring the wild and beautiful Kimberly region with some big supermarkets. If you have a 4WD you should take **Gibb River Road** through the Kimberly outback. It's a mostly unsealed road and can be difficult to pass due to bad weather conditions. So, if you explore the Kimberly bring food and water for at least a week in case you get stuck. If you only have a 2WD car, take the Great Northern Hwy toward the Northern Territory. The distance is longer than Gibb River Road but it's on normal roads and therefore easier and faster to drive and still, there are some cool things to see. More about that on the next pages, first some more info about Broome.

4.23.1 What to do in Broome

Unfortunately, Broome is a rather expensive city and therefore not really a backpacker town. However, it's still a good place to spend two or three days.

Cable Beach

Broome is famous for Cable Beach which is a huge stretch of white sand, enclosed by red rocks with a wonderful aquamarine ocean in front of you. Here, you can enjoy some of the most beautiful sunsets on earth and why not do it **from the back of a camel**? Cable Beach is 22 kilometers long. You can swim safely during the dry season, from May to October. In the wet season, unfortunately, deadly stingers may be in the water. Also, if you like **surfing**, that's possible here in Broome (beach break), especially during cyclone season.

Pearls

One of Broome's flourishing industries is the pearl industry. You can look at the pearls in one of the display rooms or even do a tour to the oyster farms.

Dinosaurs

After a ten minutes-drive out of town, you reach **Gantheaume Point Beach**. This is the departure point for Broome's kayak tours, whale watching tours (June to October), fishing charters, and extended cruises. However, the most interesting sight there is a dinosaur footprint which is well-preserved in the rock and is more than 130 million years old. You find it, by taking the well-worn track at Gantheaume Point Cliffs and lighthouse. Walk past the interpretive sign to reach the cast of dinosaur footprints. This is a popular attraction for children. The real dinosaur footprints can be seen at very low tide at the bottom of the cliff.

Asian Culture

Broome has one of the biggest Asian communities outside of China and Japan. You will encounter many Asian restaurants, or you could visit the historic Japanese cemetery and discover over 700 gravestones made from colorful rocks.

Markets
Shop for handmade jewelry, clothing and delicious street food at the Saturday (all year round) and Sunday (April to October) **Courthouse Markets**. A special treat is the **Staircase to the Moon night market** which is held over the two nights of the full moon from June to October at the Town Beach Reserve.

To travel toward the **Northern Territory** from Broome, you have two options.

4.24 First Option: Gibb River Road

This road used to be a true adventure and only for experienced 4WD drivers. However, that has changed in the past years. Gibb River Road is now usually in excellent condition and big parts of it are sealed. There are bridges over some creeks and other creek crossings have been reinforced with concrete. However, Gibb River Road is only open from April to October in the dry season. During the other months, it's closed. Especially in the main tourist season when the creeks are low Gibb River Road won't be a problem. You might not even have to put your car into 4WD. The start of the season (April to June) is a different story. When the Gibb River Road first opens there is still a lot of water in the main river crossings. Some of the creeks on the side tracks can also be very deep. In the first few weeks, you may need to be able to drive through more than 500 mm of water. Then, you need a big 4WD with a snorkel. All in all, you do need to know how much water your vehicle can handle. Yet, there is no way to predict water levels ahead. If you plan to travel in April/May, for smaller cars even June for 2WD you need to keep an eye on the current conditions of the road. Ask the rangers or police in a city in the top part of Western Australia or the Northern Territory or search the internet for current road conditions.

To avoid the danger of your tire being punctuated, drive slowly (not more than 60 km/h in rocky sections), and reduce your tire pressure before you head off-road. Recommended pressures vary depending on the size of the vehicle and the load. If you are unsure you could ask the mechanics working at a gas station. In addition, carry a spare tire in your car.

Gibb River Road is a cattle route and many long road trains drive along this road. Usually, there's too much dust from those road trains to see far enough ahead and it's safer not to overtake them.

You don't need a permit to drive in Gibb River Road or to see any of the usual attractions. However, if you want to visit **Kalumburu Aboriginal Community** you have to organize a permit before you start driving. The entry permit can be purchased online (https://aapapermits.microsoftcrmportals.com/) for free and will take about two days until it's processed.

Camping is only allowed in designated areas.

And now, to take your last fear away; along the whole road, there are many street signs. You couldn't get lost if you tried!

Must see stops along Gibb River Road

Windjana Gorge National Park

Windjana Gorge is one of the best places in Australia to see freshwater crocodiles in the wild. Lennard River cuts through the gorge and you'll see diversified birdlife and crocodiles sunning themselves near waterholes. As a hike, you could take the **Gorge Walk**, which begins at the camping area and winds through the gorge for 3.5 km each way but there are some shorter walks as well. A 4WD is recommended to access the national park.

Lennard River Gorge

Lennard River Gorge is about a 1.5-hour drive away from Windjana Gorge. Follow the two-kilometer walking track from the car park along a creek line, up to the King Leopold sandstone until you reach a lookout. From there you have a dramatic view over the gorge and waterfalls. The track to the car park only for 4WD.

Bell Gorge

Bell Gorge is very picturesque and therefore one of the most popular gorges along Gibb River Road. At the head of the Silent Grove Valley, Bell Creek drops 150 meters into a deep pool surrounded by ledges and sheltered by rocky walls. It is great for swimming.

Galvans Gorge

This is the most accessible gorge along Gibb River Road and a fun one to take a dip. You can swim in Isdell River, swing over it on a rope or simply sit under the waterfall.

Mitchel River National Park

Mitchel Falls are possibly the most beautiful waterfalls in Australia and therefore enjoys many visitors although it's a bit of a drive to get there (allow two days simply to reach Mitchel Plateau and drive back and 4WD only). It's well worth it but, unfortunately, since 2018 you need a permit to access Mitchell Plateau. Ngauwudu Road Zone Pass is valid for five days and costs $45 **per person**. You can also buy the pass online (www.wunambalgaambera.org.au/uvp-single-person-packages/uvp-independent-ngauwudu). About 60 km along Kalumburu Road you find Drysdale Homestead. Here you can get meals, fuel, ice, and basic supplies. After that, you need to be self-sufficient. The Mitchell Plateau Track is called track for the reason because it's a non-supervised road and therefore can be in a very bad condition. Find out beforehand what this means for the insurance of your car.

If this sounds like too much work and you have the necessary cash, you could also take a mesmerizing scenic flight over Mitchell Falls from Drysdale (www.drysdaleriver.com.au/scenic_flights.htm).

Mitchel Plateau Track is 85 kilometers until you reach Mitchell Falls Camping area (rangers will be there from about May to October and can help you with questions). You should allow two to three hours for this section. Only a few kilometers past the turn-off you will come across the biggest obstacle on this track: King Edward River Crossing.

Mitchell Falls Camping area doesn't have any showers, but you can collect water from the stream and there are toilets. In case you changed your mind about taking a flight after having visited the falls on foot, you can book a helicopter tour at the campground. Or, you can walk one way and the pilot will collect you at the top of Mitchel Falls in the afternoon.

The amazing hike to the falls will take you four to six hours return. It's rough terrain and there are many sidetracks to explore as well. The walk starts at the campsite and there is an info-panel explaining you some facts about the area.
First, you have to cross the pretty **Mertens Creek** which would also be a good place to have a relaxing bath in the evening. Fifteen minutes later you will be at **Mertens Falls**. Be careful near the edge! You can cross the falls at the top and will find several natural "bathtubs" where you can enjoy a soak. However, before getting to Mitchel Falls, follow the river on the right side and follow the path to your left after climbing down a small rock face. It will lead you to a cave below the falls.

The next stop is **Mertens Gorge** which also is a waterfall. A huge one but not as big as Mitchell Falls. To get to Mitchell Falls you have to cross Mertens Gorge at the top and continue on the other side. From now on, the walk is more difficult. It's a very rocky terrain with big boulders to climb over and small gravel which could make you slip quickly (wear good shoes). However, **Mitchel Falls** are just around the corner now. The cool thing is that you arrive at their top and have an amazing view over Mitchel River. Stand there, spellbound and take in the sight and the thunder of the falls. Continue on the path and then you have to cross the falls again. On the other side, you reach the helicopter-pad. From there, the path is well marked with arrows until you reach the photo lookout. If you still have energy, you can take the path before the photo lookout which leads to the left. It's not easy to get down there but you will reach the bottom of the falls. Here you are much closer to the falls and can feel their spray. However, it's not possible to swim as this is a sacred sight and salt-water crocodile terrain! Anywhere above Mitchel Falls, it should be safe as long as you don't go over a waterfall.

El Questro Homestead

I only mention this stop for the horse lovers among you as you can have nice rides in the outback at El Questro Homestead. In addition, they offer deluxe accommodation and bush camps. From here it's only 33 km more to reach the end of Gibb River Road.

Drive on to the last city along the border of WA, **Kununurra**. It's a hip small town with a big supermarket. Afterward, you will enter the Northern Territories. However, the next stretch on the Great Northern Hwy is another long one and will take you about 6.5 hours to get to Katherine.

4.25 Second Option: Purnululu National Park

In case you don't have so much time to do Gibb River Road or only have a 2WD, use the Great Northern Hwy to get from Broome to **Kununurra**. This route is less spectacular but it's all on sealed roads and you will pass the dramatic looking **Bungle Bungle Range** in Purnululu National Park. In my opinion, they look like sombrero tops growing out of the earth.

5 What to see in the Northern Territory (NT)

The NT offers the most amazing, kitsch sunsets, beautiful waterfalls, ancient Aborigines history and generally a stunning nature. It's a bit hard to get here by car but easy by plane and should not be skipped. Exploring the top end is amazing and you could spend weeks in the many national parks. The good thing about the spectacular national parks in the NT is that most of them are free. Right now, I'm only aware of Kakadu being priced at $40 per adult during the dry season and Uluru - Kata Tjuta National Park (Ayers Rock and Olgas) has an entry fee of $25. So, rent a car in Darwin or join one of the tours and start exploring.

5.1 Darwin

Darwin is the capital of the North but small and friendly enough that you quickly will feel like an inhabitant yourself.

5.1.1 From the airport to the CBD

- A taxi will cost around $25 to $30 (15-20 mins)
- Buslink (public bus) $3-$7 per person one way (60-90 minutes)

5.1.2 What to do in Darwin

Swim in the lagoon

All year round it will be hot in Darwin. However, due to the danger of crocodiles, you can't swim in the ocean. Therefore, they built a free lagoon and although the water looked a bit murky when I was there, it was a welcome refreshment.

Take a walk at the botanical gardens

They are small, but you get to see local plants. The big plus is the nice café. In addition, there is an air-conditioned info house with free Wi-Fi.

Have dinner at Mindil Beach Markets

Those famous sunset markets are a must. There are a lot of booths with handmade things to buy. It will be crowded with people, live music and the smell of good food. And all this in the soft light of the setting sun. Afterward, you will be convinced that you just saw the most beautiful sunset ever.

Have a drink at the Ski Club

I first thought they just try to be funny with the name until I realized that they meant waterski. This is an outdoor bar at the ocean on green grass, under palm trees. They often have live music. On top of that, it's a good place to experience one of Darwin's enchanting sunsets (fewer people than at Mindil Beach).

Have a night out

Darwin is a backpacker-friendly town which means there will be lots of young people out partying and with good music and glow paint everybody generally is in a great mood.

5.1.3 How to tour the NT

It's doable to explore the NT with a group of people in your own car. However, I was tired of looking for people who would travel with me and therefore signed up for a group tour. I can fully recommend **Wayoutback Tours**. They took great care of us and made sure everyone had a good time.

5.2 Litchfield National Park

About 1.5 driving hours from Darwin you reach Litchfield NP. The roads start to look more like dirt again and build an orange-red contrast to the sky. The best thing; beautiful Litchfield NP is still free to visit!

Buley Rockhole

This is a clear stream, flowing over rocks, building several swimming pools and waterfalls. It looks incredibly beautiful. Plus, the water has the perfect refreshing temperature. It's a lot of fun to fight against the currents of the waterfalls and then float back to the edge of the pool.

Florence Falls

From the viewing platform, those two broad waterfalls look amazing! One might think that you took your perfect picture with a drone…The hike down to the pool is an easy walk and takes less than 5 minutes. It's worth to jump in the water which shines green against the rock but is crystal clear too. The view from when you are floating on the back, looking up at the falling water is indescribable. On the sides, the water pressure isn't that hard and it's possible to have anice shower.

Wangi Falls

From the parking lot it's again only a very short walk to the waterfalls. Again, I couldn't take my eyes off them, they were so stunning!! Amazing colors and this big amount of water! Litchfield is a point for the bucket list for waterfall-lovers.

5.3 Murray River

Katherine Gorge is famous for river cruises but another beautiful place to take a boat tour is Murray River. On a two-hour tour you will see several big saltwater crocodiles and also some freshwater crocs. We even saw a baby crocodile! Plus, there were a lot of birds and water lilies.

5.4 Kakadu National Park

There now is an entrance fee to Kakadu NP, depending on the season of the year. However, don't let the money stop you. I couldn't pick between Litchfield and Kakadu NP, you have to do both because they are both unique.

Ubirr Rock

One of the special sights in Kakadu NP is Ubirr. It's a small, sacred mountain from which you have an amazing view! On the way to the top, it's like an outdoor museum with ancient wall paintings. Here, it's nice if you have a guide who tells you stories about the paintings and explains the rules to you about how to behave on such a sacred site. Take your time with the walk so that it's not too exhausting in the heat.

Gunlom Falls

On the drive here I spotted wild donkeys, a wallaby, and a wild pig, so be sure to look out of the window while the driver has to concentrate on the 4WD road. At Gunlom, we hiked for 20 mins up a steep path over slippery and uneven rocks. On the top, you will have a stunning view across the plain. Apart from that, you are now standing at the top of the waterfall, which looks like a natural infinity pool. The current along the edge wasn't strong and it was possible to take amazing pictures.

If you don't want to take the hike to the top upon yourself, you can also just relax at the bottom pool.

5.5 Kathrine Gorge

If you took Gibb River Road or the Great Northern Hwy from Broome, Kathrine is where you will arrive. So, from here, you can either continue north to **Darwin** or south to **Alice Springs**. Since we've now been to the top end already, we concentrate on Kathrine Gorge and will head south afterward.
At the visitor center (bless the a/c) there is a nice exhibition about the area. You can book boat tours through the gorge for about $80 or take some walks. For example, you can hike to the top of the gorge from where you will have stunning views over the water and the rocks. However, in this heat, you have to earn every meter. Luckily, at the top, there is a water tap with cold (!) water. The water is pumped up from underground that's why it stays cool.
Edith Falls is another nice place to see in Nitmiluk National Park. However, after having seen other waterfalls in the NT and WA those weren't so special and therefore could be skipped.

In Kathrine, there is a shopping center where you can stock up on goods and enjoy the free WIFI.

5.6 Mataranka

Although we had a look at the pretty **Mataranka Hot Springs** we didn't swim there because our tour guide said that those were a man-made place. Instead, we went to the **Bitter Springs** 3 km out of town which is an incredibly beautiful color spectacle. Go there early in the morning when the air is still cold because the water temperature is naturally heated to 34° C. It is a beautiful blue creek in a palm tree forest. The only downside was the many big spiders which had put up their nets across the water. I just pretended to be a crocodile and kept my head half in the water.

5.7 Daly Waters Pub

This is the oldest pub in the Northern Territory and has a very cool set up. It's filled with things that people leave behind as well as funny signs. Also, the food and drinks were cheaper than in Darwin. A good place for a lunch break.

5.8 Devils Marbles

The marbles are granite rocks that were shaped into round and oval boulders over the years. This is definitely a place to get out of the car and take a walk. Have some fun with taking pictures in between those giant Easter eggs!

5.9 Wycliffe Well

Just another stop along this long stretch of road toward Alice Springs which makes it fun to get out of the car. Wycliffe Well was one of the funniest places I've ever been to. They call it the UFO capital of Australia and everything is in an alien theme.
Now, it's not far to Alice Springs and on the way there you will cross the Tropic of Capricorn line. Not everyone can say this about having done that in their lives…

5.10 Alice Springs

Alice Springs, I couldn't believe I actually made it here. To the red center of Australia. It was a long but exciting and amazing journey (and I'd do it again).

Royal Flying Doctor Service

In Alice Springs, you can easily walk around town and you can visit the famous Royal Flying Doctor Service which operates in the outback.

Botanical Gardens

Here you'll find mostly bushes and dry, dusty or rocky soil but there also are colorful parrots and butterflies.

Shops and restaurant

You can find a wide variety of stores (K-Mart, Coles, Woolworth), restaurants (Thai, burger, fish and chips,…), and coffee shops here. The culturally interested can find several aboriginal art galleries.

Sunset at ANZAC hill

Once more you could opt to do a camel tour at sunset. You don't see Uluru from here though and, therefore, climbing ANZAC hill seems the better option. It only takes 3 mins to walk up the hill, if you take the steep path. At the top, you can enjoy a stunning sunset with an impressive view across Alice Springs, the flat desert in front of it, and the mountains behind it.

5.11 MacDonnell Ranges

The MacDonnell Ranges are rock hills which build a long chain. The gorges with green rivers are scenic, however, if you've seen any other outback gorges (for example Katherine or Karijini) this one can be skipped.

5.12 Ayers Rock (Uluru)

If you thought by flying to Alice Springs, you have reached Australia's most famous red rock, you are wrong. You have to drive another 500 km until you catch the first glimpse of it. But as they say, the journey is just as much as the destination and the red center is worth it. On the way to Uluru, you can already see a big flat mountain which people often mistake to be Uluru. That's why the tour guides call it Fooloru :) You now won't make that mistake.
Still, this tabletop mountain and then Uluru as well look quite cool in the otherwise flat landscape.
Plan at least an hour to look around the **visitor center** at Uluru as it is quite informative. There is a great movie about the Aborigines living here and a lot of art and information.
What you should do next is take the walk around Uluru, wowing at the steep, red rock. You could even hire a guide who tells you stories from the Aborigines. It's just a pity that there is a metal fence running to the top, where you could climb it on certain days. Think

about climbing it thoroughly. Uluru is a sacred site to the Aborigines and there are enough high platforms you can climb in Australia. Uluru doesn't need to be one of them. Soon, it might even be prohibited to climb on top of Ayers Rock, and they can take away the 'scar' of Uluru. There actually was an 'I did not climb Uluru' guestbook, which I found a funny idea.

Of course, you have to watch the **sunset** with the setting sun behind Uluru and the whole landscape being painted orange.

> **Tip:** Bring a warm jacket to your red center trip at any time of the year. Even though the sun was shining all day, it took ages to warm up and cooled down quickly. I was glad that I had my down jacket.

By the way, you need a park-pass to visit **Uluru-Kata-Tjuta National Park**. You can buy it online (https://book.parksaustralia.gov.au/passes/uluru/) for $25 per person.

5.13 Kata Tjuta (the Olgas)

Kata Tjuta means "many heads". All those mountains look great from a distance but also amazing up close to walk around. The rocks are fascinating, and you have the choice between different walks:

- Karu lookout: This track has some loose rocks to negotiate. Mind your step and wear good footwear. The view is breathtaking and worth the little effort. 2.2 km return, 1 hour, drinking water available at the start of the track.

- Karingana lookout: This path takes you down into the valley and to the creek beds. It is challenging in sections with many steps and some steep drops, but very enjoyable as well. 5.4 km return, 2.5 hrs.

- Full circuit walk: The remainder of the Valley of the Winds walk takes you far away from everyone and everything and into the heart of this land. This is a beautiful and enjoyable walk and I'd recommend taking this one. 7.4 km full circuit, 4 hrs. Commercial photography is not allowed. Water is available halfway along the track.

5.14 Kings Canyon

This is another beautiful place to have an amazing view across the Australian outback. The main thing to do at Kings Canyon is the **Kings Canyon Rim Walk**. It's best to do it in winter between May and September. In the Australian summer it can get very hot (38-42 degrees Celsius. That's over 100F). Therefore, if you do it in summer, start early in the morning, so that you could be back down before 10 a.m. Rangers often have to rescue people who are too exhausted during the summer months. Another danger at Kings Canyon is that people fall off any die because they take selfies. Unfortunately, that happened on the day before I was there and so half of the walk was closed. The full circuit is about six kilometers and takes three to four hours. Up to the canyon, it's about a thousand steps. Just take your time and enjoy the view. You can enjoy seeing the opposite part of the canyon and the plain around it. If you need to refresh yourself, you can take a dip at the **Garden of Eden** billabong.

5.15 Camel farm in Yulara

Yulara is the place to go on a sunset camel ride in the outback and see Uluru at the same time. Find more information here: www.ulurucameltours.com.au/.

6 Across the South: Nullarbor Plain

Norseman is the last town before the long Eyre Hyw and consists of two gas stations, an information center and maybe eight houses. So, I'd recommend that you buy all the supplies you need to get through the three days of driving the Nullarbor Plain in the biggest city before that.

Along Eyre Hyw you find a roadhouse about every 180 km though and don't have to go hungry. Gas is available at those stations as well, but it was the most expensive fuel I had to pay in Australia. Eyre Hyw is quite busy and therefore you don't have to fear being stuck and not rescued in case your car breaks down. The bigger danger is that you'll fall asleep on the wheel because it's the longest straight road in Australia (1100 km) and therefore, take enough breaks on roadside stops and bring good music to sing along to.

I had some of the best sunsets while driving across the Nullarbor Plain. The sky was golden, red and pink and this all the way to the horizon over endless fields and trees.

You can spend the nights at a roadhouse or just camp on a rest area.

Tip: Take a rest stop which leads a bit away from the highway so that you won't be bothered by road trains at night.

Eucla is a nice place to stop. They even have a pool and there, the gas was a bit cheaper as well. Somewhere, a sign announces that you must change the time 45mins (?!) ahead and then later, you have to adjust the clock again.
Before I knew it, I reached **Ceduna** and with that civilization (the gas station before Ceduna was actually a little cheaper than the ones in Ceduna).

I've seen many people who were driving this road alone and I guess it's a good experience to be on your own with just your thoughts for a few days.

Right before Ceduna, there is a **food-checkpoint**. You are not allowed to import any fruit or vegetables and if they stop you, they will take any tomatoes, apples, etc. you still have away from you.

At least, I could reward myself with a dozen oysters at the Oyster Bar in Ceduna ($8.50) after I lost all my snacks.

6.1 Adelaide

Adelaide is the capital of South Australia and the gate to some well-known wine regions. Read on to find out what else you have to see or do in and near Adelaide.

6.1.1 How to get from the airport to the CBD

- By taxi: It will take about 15 minutes and cost between $25 and $32
- By Airport City Shuttle: This is a door to door service costing $10 per person
- By double decker metro bus: It takes about 18 minutes and costs $3.50 - $5

6.1.2 What to do in Adelaide

Botanical Gardens

This botanical garden is very beautiful. No wonder that about five wedding parties were out and about to take pictures or have an aperitive. Beware that the water lily pavilion and the rainforest hall close at 4 p.m. Either way, this park is a nice place to take a walk or go read a book.

Glenelg Beach

You can take the tram to this pretty little seaside town. It's a lovely place to take a stroll or go for a swim and there are plenty of options to find lunch or dinner.

Visit a museum

Like in other Australian cities, most museums in Adelaide are free. I went to the **migration museum** which was quite interesting but too many sings to read on such a beautiful day which would better be spent outside.
I loved the **National Museum of SA**. In there you can find aboriginal art, all kinds of stuffed animals, and hunting gear.

Port Adelaide

At the red lighthouse in the harbor, the famous **Sunday Market** is located. This is a flea market with lots of things you don't have space for as a tourist but perhaps could use as a work and traveler. Another option is a **Dolphin Cruise** (you take a boat up the river to the beginning of the ocean and back again for 1,5 hours). They cost only $8 per adult and we were a bit skeptical how anything could be so cheap in

Australia. Like I thought, we then didn't see any dolphins (probably, the chance for that is very slim) but it's still a relaxing ride, observing the other ships and the birds.

Go wine tasting

You will probably recognize the following names as wine regions because they are famous all around the world. Do a self-drive tour to some wineries or hop on a guided tour from Adelaide. **Barossa Valley** is above all known for their Shiraz grapes. In **McLaren Vale**, you find tasty dry red wines. In the **Adelaide Hills,** you find a former German settlement and therefore besides wine, also beer. In addition, there are two wildlife parks in which you can cuddle with koalas. **Clare Valley** offers you more wines, historical buildings, and a big outdoor maze.

7 What to do in Victoria

Victoria is a state in the south-east corner of Australia and is home to my favorite city in Australia; **Melbourne**. It's the most densely populated state and like the other corners of Australia, has its own treasures to offer.

7.1 Great Ocean Road

Before we even start the Great Ocean Road, I will talk about a few places near the west end of the Great Ocean Road which are worthwhile to visit as well.

7.1.1 Portland

There is a nice lighthouse to which you can walk up for free and have beautiful views of the ocean. The great thing during our visit was that there were dolphins and seals playing around in the water below us.

7.1.2 Mt Eccles

The most famous mountain group in this region are the Grampians. In **Grampians NP** you can enjoy hiking, pretty views, and MacKenzie Falls. However, just before our visit there had been a big bushfire and therefore the locals recommended us to go to Mt.

Eccles, which is a dead volcanic crater, filled with a lake. Sounds exciting, right? We thought so too, and so went to check it out and weren't disappointed. Already when pulling into the parking lot we saw quite a few kangaroos jumping out and about. Walked up to the rim from where we had a stunning view! Then, we embarked on a two-hour circle hike, passing a cool cave called "Natural Bridge" and a kangaroo skeleton along a track called "Lava Canal". We saw a lot of bushland and birds. Five minutes from the car park at the other end of the walk, we reached another huge cave. Bring proper torches with you. Otherwise, you won't see a thing…

7.1.3 Warrnambool

Near here is the official start/end of the Great Ocean Road. In case you like history, you should stop here because there is a re-built historical village behind the visitor center. We thought it was quite expensive though.

Already the first lookout point along Great Ocean Road gave the view over impressive pillars in the beautiful ocean. We stopped at every lookout point after that, finding beautiful bays with intensely blue and green water. Toward the evening, we reached **Port Campbell** with free Wi-Fi at the visitor center.

7.1.4 Twelve Apostles

The next day started with the highlight from the Great Ocean Rd; the Twelve Apostles. The car park is on the opposite side of the street and then you take an underground passage to get over to the viewing platform. The view was great but, in my opinion, some other rocks along the coast looked just as impressive. It's probably just all the tourists who make them so famous.

7.1.5 Gibson Steps

This is definitely a must do stop to stretch your legs and look at the landscape in awe. Climb down to the beach and walked along the sand. From down here, the limestone cliffs look massive!

After that, we meet surfers at all the bays we stop, although there usually is a "no swimming because it's dangerous" sign…

7.1.6 Cape Otway Lighthouse

On the drive to the Cape Otway Lighthouse, we saw all these people starring up at the trees. Soon, we realized that the trees were filled with koalas hanging in the branches. So many koalas in the wild, how cool!!! However, if you are on a tight budget you might only drive part of the way to the lighthouse as it costs $17 to get close to it and take pictures.

On the other hand, it's worth stopping for at least one of the waterfalls along the way.
The 15-mins walk to Sheoak Falls in Lorne was beautiful and adventurous and the fall with its black water amazing!

A little down the road, there was another lighthouse we could walk up to and with that, I guess we've reached the end (or start) of the Great Ocean Road because there was a big gate with a sign. This and Gibb River Road are probably the two most exciting road trips you can do in Australia.

7.2 Melbourne

Melbourne or Sydney, that is the question. If you ask people about their favorite city in Australia, it's either Sydney or Melbourne. If you ask a European, often it is Melbourne. Perhaps, because it has a European feel to it or just because everything in Melbourne is awesome...It has it all from beautiful architecture, delicious and cute coffee shops, historical trams and much more.

I drove into Melbourne after two months of road tripping through West Australia and then the South and this was kind of the first big city I had seen in a long time. It was impressive to drive over the harbor and then see the huge cruise ships. The hostel we landed in was a highlight as well because they had free breakfast, free pasta, rice, and free lockers. Plus, the big lockers were free as well and that all at $24 per night. The facilities were clean and the people friendly, that even in this big hostel, it had a homey feel to it. I can fully recommend **Urban Central** hostel.

7.2.1 How to get from the airport to the CBD

- Taxi: A taxi to the CBD costs about $55 to $65 for up to four people and will take about 20 minutes.

- SkyBus: This bus leaves every 10 minutes 24/7 and will bring you in 20 mins to **Southern Cross** Station in the CBD. One way is $18.

- Public bus and tram: This is the cheapest way to get from Melbourne airport to the CBD. Purchase a **Myki card** at the Skybus Terminal, before you proceed to Terminal 1's platform. Take bus number 901, get off at **Broadmeadows Station** and then switch to a train/tram to whichever destination you have in mind.

7.2.2 What to do in Melbourne

Join the free walking tour

Once again, I had a very positive experience on the free walking tour in Melbourne. The tour guides are funny and have great stories to tell. The tour starts every day at 10.30 a.m. and 2.10 p.m. at the statue of Sir Redmond Barry in front of the State Library of Victoria.

Visit the library

Entering the state library is free and I was very impressed by this building that I put it high on the must-see list of Australia. In case you read my fantasy series **Heart of Power** you might recognize that The Library was inspired by this.

Take in the architecture

Take a walk in the city and marvel at the amazing architecture. There is not one street without a special house or bridge on it. Then, there are all the graffiti or the street art on the walls in sometimes very narrow laneways. I think, Melbourne is best visited on foot or by bicycle because that's the only way to find the interesting things in the small laneways.

Take the circle tram

If you're tired of walking, hop on the free old-fashioned city circle tram, which drives around the city center (to all my Swiss readers, did you know that in German "das Tram" is called "DIE Tram" because of DIE Strassenbahn? Sounds so wrong.) A tape informs you about all the touristy places. Therefore, it's a good idea to take the tram on your first day in Melbourne, so that you get a good overview of the city.

Go to a museum

In case it's raining, visit the museums! I was surprised to find that the Swiss artist Pipilotti Rist is so popular here. Both the **Art Gallery** (cool fountain along the building) and the **Museum of Contemporary Art** (great, cheap coffee cart at the entrance) were free. So even if you aren't usually interested in art, just give it a try :)

If you like movies, the **ACMI film museum** is a must. They have a paid exhibition which is changing from time to time and there is a permanent exhibition which is free (and so much fun!). If you want to go to the free exhibition, just walked past the waiting line of people and go directly to the free part of the museum. That was one of my favorite exhibitions ever! I went there twice so that I wouldn't get tired of looking at the things, read, listen and interact. There were old projectors, the history of movies, actors, producing, special effects and so much more. There even was a section with old video games (that's where you could find all the dads and sons). Worth a visit! And it's on **Federation Square**, which is a nice place to look at anyway.

Eat delicious meals

The restaurants in Melbourne are top notch. While usual meals are normal Australian prices I found a real gem in the **Causeway Lane** off Burke St. It's called **Sushi Monger** and at lunchtime, it will always be packed with people. No wonder, the sushi there was one of the bests I ever had, and they offer a lunch deal (2 rolls and a miso soup for $5). You might have to wait 15 mins until you can order.

Shop at Victoria Market

This market is famous, and I loved Victoria Market. I found cheap vegetables and the cheapest souvenirs, in case you have space in your luggage.

Drink a coffee

In Melbourne, I had at least one coffee at a different place every day although I'm usually not really a coffee drinker. There are a lot of cute cafés, that offer cheap ($3.50 to $5.50 for a mocha or iced coffee), delicious and beautifully crafted coffees, so it would almost be a shame to go to Starbucks (I think Melbourne and Sydney are the only cities with a Starbucks in Australia. Plus, they opened the first H&M of Australia in Melbourne in 2014. A continent without H&M, I didn't know that still existed.)
Degraves Ln and Center Place were the most central places for coffee, but I really liked the cute places along **South Wharf** and my favorite was **Phamish** in St. Kilda.

Ride a blue bicycle

When you don't want to lose too much time walking or need to go further, rent a blue bike. It's only $2.80 a day or $8 a week (you pay by credit card) and I found them perfect to ride to and from St. Kilda (go along the lake in **Albert Park**) or to ride along the water in **Docklands** or to the other suburbs in Melbourne. In the CBD, I preferred walking because it's up and down and there are too many people and cars.

Go to the cinema

In case you have been reading my blog (www.swissmissontour.com), you know that I like to go to movie theaters in different countries. On Monday, **Carlton Cinema Nova** in Melbourne offers a $10-deal.

7.3 St. Kilda

St. Kilda is the closest town to Melbourne with the prettiest beach front. It has a relaxed holiday vibe to it and in the evening, you get to see penguins at the dock.

How to get to St. Kilda

Take a blue bike from Melbourne's CBD and ride Lakeside Drive along Albert Park. So, the whole ride, there is a beautiful lake and a green park on the left and the approaching skyscrapers in front of you. In 20 minutes, you'll reach St. Kilda. Or, take tram 16, 96, 12 or 3 but they take longer than the bicycle.

What to do in St. Kilda

Enjoy a cup of coffee or a delicious meal at a restaurant along the waterfront. The choice of cute cafés, bars, delicious cake shops or restaurants is endless.
There is a small **Luna Park** which younger kids will enjoy. However, the most awesome sight in St. Kilda are the little **penguins** which climb onto the rocks behind the pier after sunset. This happens every evening and unlike Philipp's Island is free to watch. Just get to the rock area behind the pier 10 mins after sunset. The little guys will start appearing about 20 mins after sunset. They sometimes came as close as half a meter to the people, which was really cool!

7.4 Philipp's Island

Philipp's Island is famous for the **Penguin Parade**. I found it overpriced and touristy and the experience in St. Kilda much more enjoyable. However, Philipp's Island is along the coastal route if you drive from Melbourne to Sydney and so, here is how I experienced it, so that you can make up your mind whether going there is worth it.

> **Tip:** Near the penguin parade there is another **chocolate factory** where you can get free samples and a delicious iced chocolate.

On a sign it said something about several thousand people (!) coming every evening to watch the penguins appear. We waited in one of the lines, paid the $26 and then proceeded to the center where you could buy expensive food and souvenirs. Everywhere were employees who reminded us that we had to pack our cameras and phones away since we weren't allowed to take pictures anymore (thanks to the people who disregarded the no flash rule over the years!).
We saw a few penguins on the walk down to the beach, which was cute. At the beach, you sit in a huge kind of amphitheater that overlooks the ocean and wait for the sun to set. There are small lamps and their light reflects on the bellies of the penguins who come out of the water in big groups and then run across the sand in the funny way they are moving. But they really are too far away to see them. It's more just the white

bellies. So, if you go there, **bring binoculars**. But the quantity of them is impressive! It got a bit better with seeing them when we walked back to the entrance about 45 mins later since you can spot the penguins all along the board walk (once you can squeeze past all the other people who are also looking at them). So, all in all, the penguins at St. Kilda were a better experience, even though there weren't as many. Perhaps Philipp Island used to be better when it wasn't as famous.

7.5 Wilson's Promotory

This is a beautiful national park with the most southern point of continental Australia. If you have time and the weather is nice it's a great place to do a few hikes and explore "the prom" for several days.

Before you enter the park, stop at **Coral Creek** to have a look at the cute "museum town". They rebuilt old houses, like it used to be during mining times and the entry is free!

In Wilson's Promotory NP you find beautiful and funny **Squeaky Beach**. There are big, colorful and round rocks growing out of the sand and with every step you take, the sand will squeak below your feet. Also, the other beaches and mountains look really nice. From the huge campsite at the southern end, you can hike to the **southernmost point of continental**

Australia. Apart from that, there are over 30 self-guided walking tracks ranging from gentle strolls to more difficult multi-day hikes.

7.6 Canberra

This isn't in Victoria anymore but actually received its own territory, the Australian Capital Territory (ACT). The story is that Sydney and Melbourne were having a long argument about which city deserves to be the capital and, in the end, to make it fair, they just chose the city in the middle of the two of them. Although there hadn't really been anything to that city. That place then grew into the Canberra as we know it today, with a huge square with the **Australian War Memorial**. This is a really good museum with interesting displays and worth a stop. Once more, as with many Australian museums, the entry is free, woohoo.

8 Explore New South Wales

This territory is distinguished by beaches for surfers, the well-known city of Sydney and some outback national parks like the Blue Mountains.

8.1 Blue Mountains

The most famous sight in the Blue Mountains area are the **Three Sisters**. These three rock pillars are located at **Echo Point**. Probably, this parking lot will be overly crowded. Then, you can try parking at **Scenic World**, which is free. The views were stunning, I couldn't stop wowing!!!

Once you are done taking in the breathtaking scenery it might be time for some exercise? Do the hike at

Giant Stairway and then wall to **Leura** from there to return on the **Cliff Walk**. This is about a 3-hour circle. With hundreds of other people, we pilgrimaged down the never-ending 900(!) steps of the Giant Stairway. They were carved into the rock and sometimes it was just normal steel stairs. It was steep at times and the views were amazing.

400m lower, we reached the bottom of the stairs and started walking on the path to the left, suddenly being alone in a rainforest. The path went up and down but was nice and I couldn't believe the people would just walk back up the same boring stairs. Nature felt pretty wild and lonely down there and therefore we were glad to have each other as company. We then reached a neat waterfall and that's where our way up began. Phew, there were mostly just stairs as well but not as vertical as the Giant Stairway.

At some point, we ran into 70-year old Henry, who lives near here and goes walking in the Blue Mountains at least once a week. He basically jogged in front of us while my legs started to feel heavier and heavier. I was very glad when we finally reached the top :)! Henry told us, that the hike to the bottom of **Leura Falls** was wonderful too and so we moved that to the next day (yes, another nice hike if you have some time). We said goodbye to Henry and then started our way back on the **Cliff Walk** (again an easy track). Every time it went downhill again, we were whining because we knew we'd have to walk it back up again. Our poor legs! They weren't used to that after sitting in the car

for so long. But the views are just so amazing, I'd do it again right away!!
And the Blue Mountains really looked more and more blue as the sun was setting. Back at Echo Point, all the tourist buses had left and now there were only about ten people left. Private view over the valley.
If you spend a night in the Blue Mountains area, Katoomba is a good place to stay. It is a very cute town that really has a holiday feeling to it.

On your second day, you should drive to **Wentworth Falls**. The earlier you arrive, the easier it is to find a parking spot in the free car park. **National Pass** hike takes about four hours and again, includes a lot of steps but it's a good decision to start at Wentworth Falls and then end up at **Conservation Hutt**. The walk was incredibly beautiful and varying. Amazing waterfalls, followed by overhanging cliffs, rainforest, more waterfalls, the path carving into the cliffs and waterfalls again. And this view! All in all, this was even better than the walk at the **Giant Stairway**.
At the restaurant Conservation Hutt, we rewarded ourselves with iced coffees and then walked the remaining 15 mins back to the car.

8.2 Sydney

When we walked around the harbor and the Opera House came in sight, I consciously realized that I was in Australia. I had seen so many pictures of this place and now it was towering in front of me! What a stunning view! Sydney is hip and modern but offers history as well. Apart from that, you find great restaurants, the amazing harbor and a famous beachfront. Australia is trying to show its best sides in Sydney.

8.2.1 How to get from the airport to the CBD

- Taxi: A taxi from the airport in Sydney to the CBD will cost you about $45-$55 and takes about 20 minutes

- Train: Airport Link offers a fast and convenient way to reach the city and suburbs. Trains run approximately every 10 minutes and the ride takes 13 minutes. The station is located at the northern end of the terminal. Buy an **Opal Card** from the station. A trip to the CBD will cost about $18.

- Bus: You can check all the routes online (https://transportnsw.info/) and see the fares for each trip. It will take you about 12 mins to get to the city center and cost around $17

8.2.2 What to see and do in Sydney

Do the free walking tour

Every day at 10.30 a.m. and 3 p.m. the free walking starts between **St Andrew's Cathedral** and **Town Hall**. The guides are funny and explain secrets about the city which you won't find out about as a normal tourist. They work on a donation basis and so at the end, you just give as much as you'd like. For 3 hours, you will look at the sights, find your way through the underground shopping tunnels, learn about the free bus 555 that runs up and down George St and then ended up below Harbor Bridge in time for sunset. Every day at 6 p.m. there is a different free walking tour which concentrates especially on the **Rocks District**. Find out more about the stops on the tours here: https://www.imfree.com.au/sydney/.

Walk around the harbor area by day and by night

The sight of Sydney harbor really is spectacular. You can walk around the terrace of the Opera House and if you can't afford tickets to a show, you could at least go inside the Opera as far as the toilets. They are nice toilets, too :). Next to the Opera, there are the botanical gardens which are nice to stroll around on sunny days.

Have a bite to eat at the famous Sydney Fish Market

At the fish market, it's most fun if you buy several different things to try. In the end, I thought I could never eat fish again, I was so full. And that with a seagull stealing one of our sashimi!! Watch out for these beasts!

Visit a museum

- **Museum of Contemporary Art:** Its location is beautiful, right at Circular Quay. The visit is already worth it even if you don't like art because you can go up to the rooftop terrace, from where you have a beautiful view on the opera house and the water. Again, they showed some pieces by Swiss artists.

- **Art Gallery of NSW:** A great gallery and worth a visit if you like art

Take the ferry to Cockatoo Island

By taking this ferry, you get a view of the opera and the harbor bridge from the water. Cockatoo Island is cool if you want to get an idea of convict times. They still have the old houses and workplaces. Ferry tickets are between $3 and $9, depending on how far you travel.

Walk across Harbor Bridge

Ride the train to Miles Point. There is a Luna Park and the **Olympic Pool**. On top of that, you are now at the other end of Harbor Bridge. Walk up the short ramp and then enjoy the view while strolling toward the city of Sydney.

Visit famous Bondi Beach

This is probably Australia's most famous beach. It's where people are surfing, sunbathing, swimming and enjoying a nice meal. Also, the cool **Iceberg rock pools** are located next to Bondi Beach. If you are tired of just laying on the sand, you can do the **Bondi to Coogee walk**. It is six kilometers long and features stunning views, beaches, parks, cliffs, bays, and the rock pools. Tamarama, Bronte, Coogee, and Maroubra offer free electric barbecues.

Watch a movie on the world's biggest IMAX screen

The IMAX with the biggest screen of the world is located in Sydney. You can book tickets online and receive the 3D goggles at the entrance. Watching the film on this huge screen was quite impressive! The action felt extremely close. The seating rows are very steep too so that nobody below you is disturbing your view.

Stroll through the shops at Queen Victoria Building

What a splendid building, from the outside as well as the inside! Apart from the shops there also are nice cafés which will make you feel as if you belong to the high-tea society of town.

8.3 Forster

If you feel like a little beach holiday head to this gem on the ocean. The water at the beach is such a light blue and so clear. There are some very nice beach campsites and beach walks you can do. Definitely a nice place to relax for a few days.

8.4 Coffs Harbor

Coffs Harbor is another place to have a holiday and not really the right place for the adventurers among you. Following you find some things you can do around Coffs Harbor.

Visit the Big Banana

The walk along the beach is beautiful and the beach inviting for a swim. It's possible to surf or just watch the surfers as well. From Diggers Beach, you can walk straight to the Big Banana. This is an oversized banana in front of a banana plantation and a famous icon of this area.
Next to Big Banana is a lolly store where you can watch them make candy. It is magical!! They shove around slacks of sugar on a hot plate. At first, they just put a red and white one together and then they wrapped another white one around it to make a thick sausage. Then, they put another layer of three colored sugar mass around it. I thought that would end up a one of this big, flat, round twisted lolly but then they started pulling on the sausage until it was only about half an inch round and then they cut it into small candies. And guess what? Happy Birthday was written inside it in red letters. How did that get there? That's how they get the melons, smileys, and raspberries in there too. Amazing! The letters are so clear after

pulling the candy from thick to long and thin. And we received a free sample of that, too.

Swim with dolphins

At Marine Magic, you can experience dolphins or seal encounters starting at $195. Find out more about possible encounters here: www.dolphinmarinemagic.com.au/dolphin-seal-experiences.

Explore the wetlands

Follow the path along the creek behind the dolphin center. Suddenly, it will turn into a wooden bridge which leads over wetlands. All this in the middle of bushes and trees. It was serene and beautiful!

Visit Forest Sky Pier

Only a short drive off the Pacific Highway from Coffs Harbor, Sealy Lookout, and the Forest Sky Pier await you. Leave Coffs Harbor and drive up through banana plantations to reach the lookout - it's open for free to vehicles during daylight hours.

The Forest Sky Pier offers magnificent views over the city and coast of Coffs Harbor. The walking tracks through rainforest, ranging from one to three hours, are worthwhile as well.

8.5 Learn how to surf

Australia's waves are inviting surfers from all over the world. If you know how to surf already, you will find plenty of waves along the East coast. If you are a beginner, you might want to take a few lessons. One of my best surf camps was **Mojo Surf Camp** at Spot X. They have good teachers and will provide plenty of delicious food for the hungry surfers. Book your stay at Mojo Surf Camp here: https://mojosurf.com/products/2-5-day-surf-stay-spot-x/

8.6 Byron Bay

Byron Bay is Australia's **party city**. We reached it at 9 p.m. and the streets were busy with people going out. However, apart from parties it also offers a beautiful **beach** and a nice **walk to a lighthouse** with the **most Eastern point of Australia**. The water below the cliff from the lighthouse is so clear and there is a big chance to spot dolphins and turtles. The café next to the lighthouse sells delicious pies in case you are hungry after the walk.

Nice places to go out are Woody's Surf Shack, which I personally found much cooler than Cocomungas. Cheeky Monkeys has a great atmosphere and cheap Happy Hour deals too. The place I liked most was the

Railway Bar. They had a live band and just a relaxed vibe.

9 What to see in Queensland

Queensland is the most populated state and with places like Gold Coast and Sunshine Coast, it's no wonder that many travelers put the destinations in Queensland high up on their Australian bucket list.

9.1 Surfers Paradise

Surfer's Paradise is very touristy, but I liked it. There are a lot of places to eat and have coffees. People say that this is the Miami of Australia. Yes, it is similar, but I'd say the beach here is a lot nicer. And there is a pretty boardwalk stretching for at least 10 km along the beach.

What to do in Surfer's Paradise

Apart from doing anything beach related you can:

Eat cheaply

Some restaurants have special deals. For example, on Monday evening you can have $3 steak at Waxy's Irish pub. Every dish you add to the plate costs another $2. It was a good steak too and they have a nice rooftop. On top of that, you should have an amazing hot chocolate at the Beach Café. They use melted Belgian chocolate and it was as good as the hot chocolate in Switzerland.

Visit several amusement parks

I had a 3-day park Pass for Movieworld, Wet n' Wild and Sea World. I love rollercoasters and so **Movieworld** was my first goal. Unfortunately, you can't compare it at all to the Universal Studios parks. None of the shows seemed interesting and the rides were rather for kids. Because the Superman coaster was closed for maintenance, there were only three roller coasters left. They were fun, and I never had to wait more than 15 mins, but I was definitely more thrilled on other rides in other parks. Perhaps, Dreamworld would have been better. After all, they have nine thrill rides.

Wet n' Wild (obviously a water park) is the biggest in Australia and everybody had been raving about it. Only, half of the park was closed FOR MAINTAINANCE when I was there. I felt like I was in the wrong film. Maybe April was not the right month to visit this theme park.

On the other hand, I was very positively surprised by **Sea World**. They have beautiful and big lagoons for their dolphins and the show was impressive and informative. The sea lion show was very funny, and the jet ski stunt show amazing! Plus, they have quite cool rollercoasters but of course, the one with the loops was closed. But the Jet Ski one was very cool! In addition, shark bay with the underwater view was amazing! I've never seen such a big shark from so close and the other fish and corals were so colorful! That part already makes a trip to Sea World worth it.

9.2 Brisbane

You realize that Brisbane is a very developed city as soon as you step off at the real coach terminal chairs, a food court, and the train station right downstairs. In addition, Brisbane belongs to the cities that look really pretty when it's dark, especially along the river. You can take beautiful walks during the day and at night.

9.2.1 How to get from the airport to the CBD

- By taxi: Passengers can expect to pay $45 - $55. This is about a 20-min drive at off-peak times
- By Airtrain: A ticket to the city center is around $23. The journey will also be about 20 mins. They also offer a transport between the international and the domestic terminal for $5. Virgin Australia travelers can take this transport for free.
- By bus: Check the website (https://translink.com.au/) for fares and interchanges.

9.2.2 What to do in Brisbane

Take a free City Hopper ferry

During the day, it's very nice to stroll along the river (River Bar also has really good coffee). A fun thing to do is to take the free red City Hopper ferry to get to **Southbank**. When the weather is nice, you could easily spend the whole weekend just in Southbank. There were a small market, nice green patches, and small rainforests to sit down and even an artificial beach. And, of course, lots of places to eat.

Dance Salsa

Every Friday Night, there are Latin Friday Nights at **Brisbane Square**. So, if you feel like an outdoor salsa party, that's the place to be. How awesome is that? Latin dancers show off their skills from 7.00 p.m., with free dance classes beginning at 8.00 pm.

Go out

Brisbane has cool venues for going out. On top of that, every bar we visited had live music on Friday! One place looked really nice from the outside, but they wouldn't let us inside because we were dressed too casually. So, we dressed up a little more the next day and then they permitted us access to the **Cloudland**. It was worth it! I felt like in fairyland. And there was live music again!

For food, I liked the Chinese/Thai/Vietnamese food in Chinatown's **Green Tea** restaurant. That was delicious, and the portions were big too!

9.3 Noosa – The Margaret River of the East Coast

Noosa is a well-known food region with several food festivals throughout the year. Apart from that, there are nice beaches, walks, and the Australian Everglades to explore by canoe.

9.3.1 What to do in Noosa

Take a walk in the national park

The walk in the national park was very pretty. On **Palm Grove Walk**, I felt like I was back in the rainforest in South East Asia.
The walk up to the Lookout Point is also worth it. It's a very, very steep walk but the houses you pass are AMAZING. Only for the rich. And finally, the view is stunning! Lucky me, I got there right in time for sunset. Since I didn't have a flashlight, I then had to jog back to the hostel. At least it was downhill then.

Go swimming or surfing

All the beaches around here look very pretty and since the Nomad's hostel offered free surfboards, we made use of them as well.

Go on a mangrove tour

This is the must-do thing here in Noosa! I did the Everglades tour with the Discovery Group Tour Company and it was amazing! One of the best days I had over here! We got picked up at 10 a.m. at the hostel and then they drove us to a jetty, where we boarded a boat with a group of elderly people. They would just stay on the boat the whole time and enjoy a lunch, whereas we would paddle up and down the creeks. For about half an hour, we drove on a big stream, and then on a lake between trees and grass, houseboats, campgrounds and the island from Richard Branson, where apparently a night costs $24'000. Then we reached a little jetty, where we had tea and very delicious baked goods. After that, our guide led us to the canoes. We were all teamed up and explained in which direction we should follow. For about an hour, we paddled along the freshwater creek. It was very serene and beautiful with the jungle on both sides of the water. Sometimes we forgot to paddle because we were enjoying the scenery so much.
We made it to our lunch destination without tipping over. On the BBQ, our guide cooked sausages, steak, and fish for us and on the table, we could find

different kinds of salad. The food was delicious and such a welcome change to my easy backpacker food. After lunch, we didn't really have time to digest, because the canoe people had to paddle ahead to make it back to the starting point in time. On the way back, we got into a Viking splash fight and a few races. In the end, we arrived soaked but since the sun was still out, that was ok. It was a lot of fun and I'd have liked to do another tour the next day.

Visit Eumundi Markets

On Wednesdays it's market time in Eumundi and since the Nomads hostel offered a shuttle service there. I'm so glad I took the opportunity to go there. Eumundi had such a great selection of food and you could sample many things. I found 10 passion fruit for $2!!! Cheaper than in Thailand. A welcome change in the expensive Noosa.

9.4 Fraser Island

This is a stop for almost every backpacker along the East Coast and so it should be! You will see incredible things and make great new friends. However, first, you have to make it through the island briefing. Prepare for three hours of torture and bring some snacks. You must watch a HORRIBLE 50min safety video that almost made me want to walk out and not do the tour just that I could stop watching that video. Finally, it was over but then we had to listen to a guy talking about the same things again, and how big the spiders would be on the island and many other unpleasant things. It really didn't sound very inviting anymore. We got divided into our groups and I ended up with two Irish girls, two British girls and a British Couple. We didn't know it then but that would turn out to be the best group from that tour. Until we all had our 4WD and supplies it took over an hour, but finally, we were ready to leave. Each car had a walkie-talkie and so we could communicate with the other cars from Brendan's group. We made the ferry in time and 20min later, we were driving on the sand of Fraser Island. Driving on all the awesome sand and forest tracks was fun and adventurous on its own and on top of that, we got to see so many cool places too.

Every group had supply boxes and a cooking box. We had heard from other groups before that there was not enough food for the trip, so we had brought all kinds of snacks. However, we received loads of food. For lunch, we always had wraps or sandwiches with a slice of cheese, lettuce, tomato or cucumber, and cold cuts. It was fun to be camping again, where we had to figure out every step because we weren't in a convenient kitchen, where we could find everything.

In the first afternoon, we did a 40min hike through a pretty forest and at the end, we were suddenly walking on a **sand dune**. Behind the sand dune, there was a beautiful, **green lake**. It could have been a quarry lake in Austria, except for the sand around it. It was a nice refreshment after the walk.

At the camp, we choose a tent for two or three people and then we started cooking right away, although it was only quarter to 5. Good idea, since there weren't many cooking spaces and my group was able to eat at a normal time, while others were still cooking at 8 p.m. in the dark.

At some point, we went to "bed". Supposedly there were foam mats under the tent and it was soft enough when I first lay down but to sleep the whole night on the naked tent floor surely wasn't the most comfortable place I had ever slept. At least it was pretty warm. I only used my silk sleeping bag.

For breakfast, we had eggs, toast and coffee/tea. We really couldn't complain! There was cereal, peanut butter, jam and toast for the next day. We had a manual for what food we were allowed to use when :).

After breakfast, we all drove to **Eli Creek**. The guides call it hangover creek because the clear fresh water has magical powers of healing headaches. We all marched along a wooden boardwalk to get to the beginning of the stream. I felt like in a water park, walking to the top of the slide. Then, like penguins, we jumped into the (at first) quite chilly water. It was wonderful floating down the stream and then ending up at the beach of the ocean. I'd have loved to do that a second time.

Then, we stopped at the **shipwreck**. Brendon told us its story and then the people who were quick managed to get a few pictures. However, it started pouring and so everybody was jumping back into the cars. Since the weather wasn't great in the afternoon, we didn't walk up to **Indian Head**. Instead, Brendan took us to a huge sand dune past the Champagne Pools, where normal tour groups with better weather wouldn't go. The dune was massive and extremely steep, but it wasn't that much different of walking up a steep hill with a lot of snow. The view from the top was beautiful but the most fun part was going back down! We all did kangaroo jumps, which means, you just jump out into the air and then land a few meters lower, where you would end up sticking in the sand. It was so much fun!

On the way back to the camp, we did stop at the **Champagne Pools**. They looked really nice, like infinity pools carved into the rocks, which would shelter them from the ocean.

The second night, we had delicious steaks, potatoes, and salad for dinner. Again, our teamwork was great and so while most other groups were still fighting for space on the BBQ, we were already roasting marshmallows around the campfire :).

We went down to the beach for a while but since it was pitch black, we didn't want to stay there for too long and end up as dingo food (after all these stories we heard…).

The next morning, we already had to pack up. I really was looking forward to a normal bed and shower but the time on the island has just been great! We had a long, bumpy but awesome drive to **Lake McKenzie**. Brendon saved this highlight for the last day and luckily, the weather finally played along. When we got to the crystal blue freshwater lake with extremely white sand, the sun was out, and the sky was clear. Everybody jumped into the water. It was wonderful!

Then, the drive back to the boat followed, which was the most exciting one because the tide came up pretty high and so our jeeps were splashing through water, our drivers doing their best, not to get stuck or washed into the ocean. It was exciting, and in the end, no problem. We drove back onto the boat, which brought us back to Rainbow Beach, where we just had to unload our cars and then finally could enjoy a real shower and clean clothes.

Then, I went out for dinner with my group. There was a good deal for pizza or fish and chips with a soft drink for $10 and the food was good too. A nice way to end our adventure!

A lot of my new friends I saw again up north since everybody follows the tourist stream. So, when I got onto the Greyhound bus to Agnes Water the next day, I knew 90% of the people on the bus. I had such an amazing time in Noosa and Fraser and I know it's above all due to these awesome people I met along the way.

9.5 Sailing the Whitsundays

Between Fraser and the Whitsundays, I spent one night in **Agnes Waters**, which is next to a place called 1770. It's a very small town but the Cool Bananas Hostel we stayed at was awesome and the beach beautiful. It would be worth to stay more than just one night and here I found the best surfing conditions for intermediate surfers. Humans weren't the only ones on the water though. There were about a million butterflies hovering over the waves.

The starting point to board the ship for the Whitsundays is **Airlie Beach**. This is another touristy place with a lot of shops, restaurants, and bars but I found it very agreeable to stay there. You can't swim in the ocean because of dangerous stingers but there is a beautiful lagoon around which you can perfectly relax, have a BBQ and swim in the saltwater pool.

Down at the docks, I learned that the Samurai would be our home for the next two nights. Since we were only 12 passengers (and two crew members) on a boat that usually fits 25 people (I really don't know how that would work though), we all had a nice amount of space.

We set out in the open sea on a beautiful day. In fact, the weather was so nice that we could only really sail without the motor for 45mins during the three days. But it was a lot of fun like that, too.

Our first stop was **Hayman Island**. The certified divers jumped into the water first and we had a nice 42min dive. Visibility was not that good but there were many fish and beautiful corals and just the feeling of floating underwater reminded me again that I really should dive more.

For the rest of the afternoon, I went snorkeling, while our skipper took a few other groups for an introductory dive. I saw about the same things snorkeling than during diving since everything was up in shallow water.

Most of the night, we spent lying on the deck, looking at the amazing sky. There were soooo many stars. We could clearly see the Milky Way and there were many shooting stars.

The next morning, we headed to **Whitehaven Beach**. We got off on the other side of the island, where it first was time for some funny pictures. Then, we walked to the stunning white beach, where we played around with the cameras some more. This beach surely was amazing! Too bad that you have to wear wetsuits to swim in the water because of the stingers. Luckily, I didn't see one.

After the beach, we hiked up to the viewpoint. The view from there was even better than being at the beach itself. That was probably the most beautiful nature panorama I have ever seen. Just such a stunning mix of blue, green and white colors!

After lunch, we went snorkeling at a different spot and for the sunset, we went to a sandbank in the middle of the ocean. We walked to one end of the island and after the sunset, we walked back and realized that part of the sandbank was under water now. Good that I wasn't wearing long pants. We even saw a turtle sticking its head out of the water and a small shark. The second night was wonderful again and the next morning, we went snorkeling around the sandbank but there wasn't much to see. Visibility was pretty bad. It was good just to be in the water and at the beach anyway. Then, it unfortunately already was time to sail back to Airlie Beach. Good music, great company, and beautiful weather made this trip perfect!

So far, Fraser and the Whitsundays (and surfing) really were the highlights of the East Coast. The beaches and colors of Whitehaven Beach and watching the stars from the boat at night should be something you should put on the top of your Australia list.

9.6 Cairns

Cairns is the gateway to the lush rainforests of Australia's North-East and also to a treasure in the ocean; the Great Barrier Reef.

9.6.1 How to get from the airport to the city center

- By taxi: A taxi to the city center will cost between $25 and $30 and will take about 15 minutes
- Backpacker shuttle: $6 to your hostel in the city center in about 45 minutes and in 90 minutes to Port Douglas for $28
- By public bus: Connect bus brings you to the public bus station in the city center for $6.20 in 15 minutes

9.6.2 What to do in Cairns

The center of Cairns is quite touristy. There is a good **shopping mall** and a **lagoon** where you can swim since, unfortunately, it's too dangerous in the ocean due to crocodiles.
The **esplanade** stretches for about 7 km (I didn't realize that and thought I would just go for a short stroll along the sea). There were nice parks, playgrounds, and outdoor work out places. Even a small boulder climbing area.

A bit further from the center but worth to visit are the **botanical gardens**. They are huge and basically a rainforest jungle, which is pretty cool. However, don't forget to put on mosquito repellent or your walk will be shortened because you have to escape from them. Do the **red arrow walk** up a hill, from where you'll have a nice view overlooking the ocean and the airport.

On Saturday, a must is **Rusty's market**. That's something you don't want to miss! We found cheap vegetables (perfect guacamole avocados for 10 for 2! I was eating avocado for the rest of my days here :)). Apart from the vegetables, you can buy delicious street food and nice fruit smoothies.

9.7 Great Barrier Reef

Tours to the Great Barrier Reef, especially the outer reef will go deeply in your pocket but for such a once in a lifetime experience, you have to scrape together the necessary cash. I booked a tour on the **Ocean Freedom** and boarded the ship at the reef fleet terminal early in the morning. I had to fill out another diving form and then could help myself to coffee, a Danish and fruit from a huge and delicious fruit plate. I found a nice seat on the upper deck in the shade.

We drove for about 1,5 hours to a dive spot called **Wonderwall**. Already the first poor people were getting sick but luckily, I wasn't affected by the waves and was ready to start the first dive when we got to the spot. We jumped off the boat into an incredible underwater world. I wished I could have stayed down there forever! The first thing I saw was a HUGE fish. At least 1m high and almost the same length as me. There were weird looking plants, some of them looked like feathers you could put on a hat. So many colorful fishes in patterns I had never seen before. They looked like candy or ice cream. And fish in such an intense blue! Plus, I saw Nemo, his sisters and brothers and cousins, and grandparents…There were so many fish! The best was, I finally got to see a turtle! And what a beauty. Moreover, we saw a second one later, that was still a baby.

It was one of the best places I have ever dived at. Unfortunately, after 40mins we were already back at the surface and made space for the introductory group dives. I jumped back into the water with my snorkel gear on. There were some schools of fish right behind the boat and a big (1,5m) barracuda with scary teeth, that would swim up really close to you because it thinks you will feed it. There were a lot of waves and so even snorkeling could make you feel a bit queasy. Luckily, back on the boat, a beeeeeautiful lunch buffet was set up.

Then, we drove to a second spot. We all hopped on a glass bottom boat and had a short, guided excursion. We hopped into the water again and snorkeled back to the boat with the slight current. It was amazing. We were somewhere miles away from the mainland but there was a sandbank in the ocean. You'd think that everywhere away from the land, the ocean would be deep. Not here. The deepest spots where the corals were was actually only about 4m deep. The water was clear and so it was the perfect conditions and place to spot fish and corals. What a beautiful place!

Too soon, we started the way back. First, they were coming around with a fruit plate again. A little later, with a cheese board and crackers!! And just as I was thinking that something sweet would be nice, they carried around a tray with different cake slices. I was so happy I landed on this boat :)!

9.8 Port Douglas

This is perhaps not a backpacker place because it has many holiday resorts where you can enjoy a few nice days. However, Port Douglas just looks pretty and romantic and therefore is worth it to at least stop for dinner and stroll along the cozy street. Otherwise, it's a good base for exploring the Daintree National Park in case you don't want to have to drive all the way back to Cairns.

9.9 Daintree Rainforest

For this tour, we rented a car in Cairns and to my dismay, it was a manual car. I'd have to drive a stick shift a whole day, with the stick on the left side!!! Considering that, I think I did pretty well :). There only was one embarrassing moment when I took about half a minute to turn the car back on at a one-way street at a construction site (it was an uphill start…). Funny was, that the indicators and windshield wipers were on the same side as in Switzerland in this car. Apparently, Australians don't know what they want.

After a 40min curvy mountain road drive, we reached **Kuranda**, which was supposed to be a similar hippie town as Nimbin, just bigger. Every day, there is a market, but it wasn't very busy. It still was worth a stop though but most of all, due to **the Barron Falls**.

They are another short drive from town. 2mins from the car park, there is a lookout with a great view over the falls. Take the nice walk to the bottom of the big falls with a refreshing swim in the pool.

Our next destination was **Mossman Gorge**. We drove straight past Port Douglas and then parked the car on the big car park at Mossman Gorge. I didn't expect this place to be that touristy! You can pay for a shuttle bus to bring you to the entrance of the gorge or you can walk for 20min on a normal road, where the shuttle buses will pass you every few minutes. We walked and came by an aboriginal community and already a few lovely creeks. There were beautiful blue butterflies, too.

The longest walk you could make once you reach the forest trails is only 45min, so we didn't really see a point for the shuttle bus.

The rainforest was very lush and green, and I loved the fern trees that looked like palm trees. The famous bridge was partially a suspension bridge. It moved when people walked on it! The water in the stream was very clear and beautiful, so I just had to jump in. Very refreshing! Then, we walked back to the entrance and had lunch at the picnic area.

Then, we had about another hour of driving ahead of us to get to the river, where we had to take a car ferry to get to Cape Tribulation. They asked $23/car for a return trip on the ferry. It only takes 2minutes to cross! Half joking, I asked the guy whether we could get it for 22$ to make it easier to split it through 4 people and to our surprise he just agreed. Then, the fun part of driving started. The roads were very windy and up and down and narrow curves through the rainforest. It was the first time since WA that it felt like being on an outback road again, where you actually had to concentrate on driving and where it rather felt like a roller coaster ride. All the (some of the quite big) holes in the ground were dangerous. I'm glad we were in a rental car, I wouldn't want to expose my own car to this road. I had a great time driving there (and that with a manual), I hope my fellow passengers did too :).

Unfortunately, we did not see one animal (except the red-headed turkeys, they are everywhere). That was a bit disappointing. We would have needed more time to find better walks but since it started raining, we just went to one beach. It was still pretty with all the mangroves in the water and Alexandra Lookout would probably be amazing on a nice day. To really see some wild-life I recommend going on a guided walk with a ranger. Find more information about guided tours and accommodation in the Daintree Forest or Cape Tribulation here:

http://rainforesthideaway.com.au/guided-rainforest-night-walks.htm.

Since we didn't want to end up in the rainforest in the dark, we started driving back by late afternoon. The ferries would cross until midnight though.

9.10 For waterfall lovers

The best about the area north of Cairns is that there are so many magnificent waterfalls. The best is, to rent a car and just go explore them for a whole day. Here is a route to catch six in one day.

Start early at around 7.30 a.m. and drive up to the **Southern Tablelands**, Take in the views of the wonderful scenery along the way. Your first destination is the small dairy town of **Millaa Millaa** where you'll explore several different waterfalls. On the Millaa Millaa waterfall circuit, you'll visit Millaa Millaa Falls which are famous from some shampoo commercials, Zilliee Falls and Elinjaa Falls. Millaa Millaa Falls are a great place for a swim and to enjoy a massage from the falling water. Don't forget to take the picture of swinging back your long hair. **Zilliee Falls** are a short walk through the rainforest and offer some great photo opportunities from the viewing area at the top of the falls. **Ellinjaa Falls** are also only a short walk away. They are particularly impressive in the wet season.

Now, jump back into your car and drive deeper into the Tablelands, making your way over lush green hills until you arrive at **Mungalli Falls**. This is the highest waterfall in the Tablelands at 90m high, with water cascading over 3 tiered levels. The fun thing in that area is the long landslide you can slide down. However, it's only open to tours and you should inquire at mungallifalls@mungallifalls.com for more information about doing the slide.

Another must-see stop is **Millstream Falls**, which is Queensland's widest single-drop waterfall. After having taken enough pictures, you make your way to the last waterfall of the day at the impressive and interesting Mt Hypipamee Crater. The crater is a deep cylindrical hole filled with water, and there are spectacular views from the viewing platform at the rim of the crater. While here you'll see **Dinner Falls**, of which the lowest tier is the most impressive.

10 A glance in the rearview mirror

Wow, we did it! Once around Australia. Several times I have been asked what my favorite place was. It's such a difficult question but I tried to make a few lists which you already saw in the Highlights section at the beginning of the book. Australia definitely lived up to my expectations or beyond it. I had amazing road trips through the outback and on never-ending straight roads. I slept below beautiful, starry nights in only a tent surrounded by nature and I was impressed by charming and modern cities with nice coffee places and delicious restaurants again and again. I hope you will have just such a great experience in Australia as I did and meet so many lovely people too. Then, you will realize that you can still have positive adventures in this world today and that our earth is a beautiful place that demands to be visited.

Things that surprise me:

- Bird whistle in much different tunes and melodies than in Europe. It sounds as if people are whistling, or a song on a radio, monkeys, or somebody laughing

- The showers have old faucets to regulate the hot and cold water (with two handles) it takes ages to get the water to the desired temperature. What a waste of water!

- There are more places without internet or phone reception than anywhere else in the world I've ever been.

- Helpful people and kind people in places we least expected them to be

- It's possible to have no McDonalds around for 2000km in any direction!! (Same for Starbucks and H&M)

- Big birds, big eagles, big fish, big kangaroos, big spiders (everything is in all sizes here!) Plus, the eyes of spiders look like diamonds in the light of a flashlight.

- Spotting koalas and possums is so awesome for people like me who get excited when they see a squirrel because I hardly ever get to see a wild animal at home

- How much rain and cold Australia gets in winter! Didn't exactly chose the right half year to travel, or did I? At least there weren't so many tourists, but my sunny Australia illusion is shattered.

- Ciders. We need to import more brands to Switzerland.

- On all the TVs in public areas, there was always a cooking show on. All the time!! Or The Voice of Australia.

- Australia has good chocolate!

- How the fuel prices can vary even during the week! From 1.34 to 1.63! It's worth to check online (at least in Perth that worked).

- That my student concession card didn't work anywhere on the West and South coast. They only accepted local cards although STA told me that the ISIC card was an Australian invention.

- Retired Australians seem to get the best discounts

- The amazing nature. Knew that before I got here but there really are extremely beautiful places and I just couldn't stop saying 'wow'.

Do you need more info?

In case you need more info, I am happy to help as far as I can. Contact or follow me through these channels:

(b) www.swissmissontour.com

(i) @swissmissontour

(f) SwissMissOnTour

(w) www.slgigerbooks.wordpress.com

Was this guide helpful?

In case you liked this guidebook, I'd greatly appreciate a positive review on Amazon. Thank you very much! Your support helps me to be able to write even more "I love…" travel guides. 😊

More books by S. L. Giger aka SwissMiss on Tour